Your Consumer Rights in Ireland

Your Consumer Rights in Ireland

Tina Leonard

LONDUBH BOOKS

First published in 2011 by
Londubh Books
18 Casimir Avenue, Harold's Cross, Dublin 6w, Ireland
www.londubh.ie
1 3 5 4 2
Origination by Londubh Books; cover by bluett; cover photo by Ronan Lang
Printed by ScandBook AB, Falun, Sweden
ISBN: 978-1-907535-20-8

Contents

Foreword

From the time you get up to the time you go to bed, your trans-áactions and the products in your home will be governed in some way by the vast array of consumer legislation on the statute books.

The alarm clock that wakes you up and the kettle that boils the water for your morning cuppa are subject to product safety rules. There are rules about the chemicals allowed in the cream you put on your face and in the material of the sofa you sit on. You choose from whom you buy your electricity and gas, your phone, internet and TV cable: all these services come with terms and conditions.

It is also prescribed by law that the food you eat is safe and that there are labels on the packaging telling you what a product contains. You hail a taxi, hop on a bus or jump on a train; yes, that's all covered too. Not to mention travelling by plane. Even your options for moving around an airport if you have mobility issues are catered for by consumer legislation.

Take a look around your home at all the products around you – your sofa, your clothes, your TV and the crockery in your kitchen. Each time you bought any of these items the retailer was promising to provide you with something that complied with the tenets of consumer law. You get the picture: we are consumers and consumer legislation permeates every aspect of our lives. Yet most of us have little idea what those rights are, which is remarkable when you consider the amount of purchasing we do and the number of contracts we enter into.

That's why I've written this book: to bring together in one place all the key elements of consumer protection that apply in Ireland. Given that the area is so broad, I've chosen topics based on the main pieces of consumer legislation and have also included tips and advice for the areas in which most problems tend to occur.

Why is consumer protection so important? Well try imagining what life would be like if there was no consumer law at all. An electrical product could be potentially hazardous. Who would know what your food contained? Who would care if your fridge stopped working, if a taxi refused to take you, if your holiday operator left you stranded abroad or if you paid for something and it was never delivered to you? Advertisements could contain a pack of lies, prices could mislead you and contracts might contain terms so harsh they beggared belief. It's not a pretty picture, is it?

That's why consumer legislation is there – to protect your interests and to redress the balance of power between you and the business you are buying from. Without it, and without knowing about it, you would not have much hope of arguing your case against a company that couldn't care less. With it, you can say, 'Actually I know what my rights are and I'm asking that you respect them.'

This is consumer power. It comes from consumer knowledge and consumer education. In a nutshell, if you're spending your hard-earned money you owe it to yourself to know what your rights are or at least where to find out about them. That way a business will never be able to pull the wool over your eyes when you are asking them to sort something out for you. Having the ability to hold your ground and say, 'You know what, I know I am entitled to this so give it to me,' puts you in a very powerful position indeed.

While this book isn't about saving money, by knowing your consumer rights you can do just that. That's because of what's called consumer detriment: the money you lose if a transaction goes wrong and isn't resolved. This detriment is very real. In 2010 Ireland's European Consumer Centre secured refunds amounting to €105,848 for Irish consumers. And this was just for cross-border purchases. Add to this the money refunded via the small claims procedure, the ombudsmen and other dispute resolution schemes, as well as money lost because consumers did nothing about their problem and you begin to have a picture of the potential financial loss I'm talking about.

When a consumer loses, their future spending power and their willingness to spend again are affected. And that affects the whole of society, including the businesses that exist because of our custom. Every time we shop we expose ourselves to this risk and now this risk of detriment has a greater consequence than before because we simply don't have as much to spend. Now that we are dealing with global as well as national suppliers, new business models and sales channels and our own leaner wallets, the system that protects us as consumers had better be good.

Thankfully there is a lot of legislative review going on right now. This year alone has seen new consumer laws on timeshare, management companies and toy safety. Proposals have been adopted for new laws on food labelling and online shopping, while reviews are under way relating to laws on goods and services, package travel and air travel – to name but some of the initiatives. Changing the law can take an excruciatingly long time and often after new legislation comes into force something new has come along in the marketplace and it's time to change it again – and so the ball keeps rolling.

There is little point in having legislation in place at all if it isn't enforced adequately. If you look at the 'Who's Who' section at the back of this book, you'll get an idea just how many agencies there are to deal with issues that affect consumers. They need to cooperate to keep their eye on the big picture and be truly effective. They also need to be proactive. Responding to a consumer problem and calling for change is easy enough: anticipating areas that require work before problems occur is less so. But that's what we need:

proactive leadership and resources used wisely and well, especially given there isn't that much money to go around these days.

Finally, never let anyone say that if you're pro-consumer you must be anti-business. Businesses and consumers are in the marketplace together and one group would simply not exist without the other. A knowledgeable consumer, a powerful one, is more likely to buy more and report positive experiences. If that's not supporting business I don't know what is.

To anyone reading who works in retail please remember: firstly, there are consumer laws you must comply with; and secondly: treat each and every one of us with respect, give us a decent service and resolve any problems that arise. When it comes to transactions things will go wrong, but it's how a business deals with the issues that marks them out as being the best. Consumers will respond with courtesy and by continuing to give you their custom.

Using this Book

Each chapter covers a specific topic so you can turn to it to find out about your rights in that particular area. At the end of each chapter I've included the names of organisations or agencies that you can turn to for advice or support on that particular topic and also details of the relevant legislation in case you need a bit of extra quoting power.

At the end of the book there is a chapter on how to complain, as in my experience the way in which consumers complain can often be a key factor in resolving a problem. Once you've found out what your rights are, you can make your complaint in an effective way. There is also a chapter explaining how the small claims system works: even with your knowledge of consumer rights and smart approach to sorting out a problem, the chances are you may need it at some stage.

I've also included a list of the government departments, organis-ations and agencies that matter in the consumer world, as a reference guide in case you ever need them. I can't claim that I have covered every single thing you'll need to know but at least with knowledge of your key rights and details of who to contact for further help, you'll have the tools at your disposal to avoid encountering a consumer problem in the first place. If you do, you'll know how to negotiate a resolution.

That is the aim of this book. Everyone can become a knowledgeable and powerful consumer – so why not go for it? One last thing: this book contains a description or interpretation of your legal rights but it is not a legal text, so should not be treated as such. That's the disclaimer out of the way.

1

Buying Goods and Services

Legislation governing goods and services covers everything from buying a coat to a car and from hiring a horse to a handyman. However, as buying cars is such a big area, this is included in a separate section (see Chapter 7).

Once you buy something, you and the seller have agreed to the terms and conditions: the price to be paid, what the product does or what the service provides and, if it is a service, how it will be carried out. Your end of the deal is to pay up. The seller has to provide what was agreed. In addition they have to provide you with your statutory rights. They cannot opt out or take these rights away from you. Your rights are pretty straightforward so what you need to do is apply them to whatever situation you find yourself in.

In this Chapter
- Your rights when buying goods
- Returning goods you don't want
- Gift vouchers
- Your rights when buying services
- Tips for buying services
- Buying services abroad
- Businesses closing down
- Who to complain to
- Legislation name check

Your Rights when Buying Goods

When it comes to buying any product your rights are covered by two main pieces of legislation; the Irish Sale of Goods and Supply of Services Act 1980 and EC Directive 99/44 on the Sale of Goods and Associated Guarantees.

The product must be:

- Fit for purpose: it works and does what it is supposed to do.
- As described: it does what it says on tin, or as per the description given to you by the sales person. Equally, if something, say a piece of carpet, is sold by sample, what you end up getting should be exactly the same as the sample you were shown.
- Of merchantable quality: the quality is reasonable in relation to the function of the product so that it doesn't break down or fall apart.

If any of the above does not apply, the seller is in breach of their contract with you. This is where the three 'Rs' come in: repair, replacement and refund.

If the washing machine spin cycle doesn't work properly or if the camera was supposed to have a video mechanism and it doesn't, you can look for a remedy. The remedy has to be provided free of charge and within a reasonable period.

(Bear in mind that you must have bought from somebody who is selling in the course of a business: these rights do not apply if you buy from a private seller.)

Buying in a sale

Your rights when you buy something in a sale are exactly the same as when you buy at full price. Just beware buying something labelled as damaged. It's your choice to buy it so you won't be able to return it, having accepted it as damaged in the first place.

Which remedy should I ask for?

This is the million-dollar question: for example, at which stage you might expect a refund rather than a repair isn't black and white. It all depends on the specifics of the situation.

As a rule of thumb the sooner the item becomes faulty the more likely it will be that you can get a refund. So if you buy something and it doesn't work at all from the start, you should get a refund – or a replacement if you prefer. Or if the product has worked for a short period and then breaks down the same should apply. That is why it is important to go back to the shop as soon as a defect becomes apparent or when you notice that the product doesn't do all it is supposed to.

Let's say you buy something and discover it's faulty, then stick it in a drawer and do not remember to do anything about it until a year later. By this time you may be deemed to have accepted the product, warts and all, so your chances of getting a full refund become slimmer.

Another thing to take into account is how long a particular product might reasonably be expected to last. Let's face it, a washing machine used for a family wash twice a day might not last as long as one used twice a week in a smaller household. You will know the answer to this question when you find yourself in a situation like this.

If you reckon the product should still be working perfectly after a couple of years, the seller is still liable to provide a remedy. In this situation you should accept a repair but after one or two repairs have been carried out, everyone should face the fact that the product needs to be replaced or a full or partial refund given.

Your rights are strongest within six months of purchase. According to EU law, if a product becomes defective within this time-frame it is understood to have been defective from the start and you don't have to prove it. However, after this time has elapsed you do have to prove the fault and the seller can send the product away for testing if they choose to.

Problems with electrical goods

One of the scenarios I hear about most frequently is that an electrical product breaks down and the customer goes back to the shop and asks for it to be fixed or replaced. Very often the retailer will send you back to the manufacturer, which all fine and large if you still have a valid manufacturer's warranty and if the warranty covers the problem.

Even though the warranty may no longer be valid, retailers still send their customers back to the manufacturers, who will charge you for repairs.

Guess what? Of course the manufacturer can charge you as they have no contract with you once the warranty is no longer valid. The retailer has a legal obligation to you and has always had. It's the retailer who is obliged to remedy the problem, regardless of whether you ever had a manufacturer's warranty or not. So don't let the retailer fob you off.

Proof of purchase

You must be able to provide proof of purchase when seeking a remedy for a faulty product or service. This could be a receipt but alternatively you could provide a debit or credit card statement.

WEEE

In 2005 new legislation (Waste Electrical and Electronic Equipment or WEEE for short) came into force with the aim of increasing the recycling of electrical and electronic goods by putting responsibility on producers and retailers. Consumers pay for it via a fixed charge that is added to the price of the item and used to fund the recycling scheme, including collection, storage, delivery to civic amenity centres, onward transportation and recycling. There are two means of disposing of your old electrical or electronic goods:

1. Civic amenity centres (there are sixty-four of these around the country) must take your old goods free of charge.
2. When you buy a new appliance you can bring your old one (regardless of where you bought it) back to the store within fifteen days and they must accept it for recycling. In the case of a big item such as a washing machine the retailer must take your old one away within fifteen days of delivering the new one.

How long do I have to make a complaint?

We are lucky in Ireland as we have six years to make a claim (the minimum protection under EU law is two years). The timeframe of six years isn't written into our specific consumer legislation on goods and services but is provided under our Statute of Limitations. That legislation imposes time limits for taking legal action and in relation to breach of contract the limit is six years.

This means that, within a period of six years, if the retailer or service-provider won't provide a remedy for something that has gone wrong, you can always take further action, for example make a claim through the small claims procedure. However, this doesn't mean that you should hang around for years before taking action. You should always make your complaint as soon as possible and take into account how long the product is expected to last, given reasonable wear and tear.

Returning Goods You Don't Want

There is a lot of confusion about this so let's get it clear once and for all. Your statutory rights to a remedy kick in only when what you buy turns out to be faulty or not as described: for example, when the heel falls off your shoe or when the chair that is supposed to recline doesn't budge.

If you want to return something because it doesn't fit or the colour of the carpet doesn't go with your curtains, it is entirely up to the shop whether they allow you to do so. Some shops have good returns policies and will offer you a refund, an exchange or a credit note if you change your mind. They will usually allow it only within a certain period, which can be shorter during sales. Other shops refuse point blank. It is up to them.

Whenever you buy anything, ask what the returns policy is. If the shop doesn't have one, don't buy there if you are not 100 per cent sure you want the product.

Gift Vouchers

A gift voucher is a product you are buying so as with any product it should do what it says on the tin. But gift vouchers should be treated like cash with an expiry date. If you lose one, it's gone forever. And if it's past the expiry date the shop is under no obligation to accept it.

There is no law that specifically governs the sale and use of gift vouchers so always check the expiry date and any conditions of use. Some vouchers don't have expiry dates at all – which is as it should be – and others businesses, such as one4all vouchers, will renew a voucher if it goes out of date in return for an administration fee.

Be on the look-out for nasty traders who start to apply a monthly charge when vouchers haven't been used after a specific period. In fact avoid them; this is a mean practice.

Your Rights When You Buy a Service

When you buy a service there are certain things you have a right to expect:

It should be carried out with the necessary skill: for example, there should not be gaps between the flooring and wall, the wallpaper pattern should match up and the dentist should know what he is doing.

- Any parts used should be of merchantable quality: for example, the pump fitted shouldn't fall apart after a few months.
- Any parts used should be as described: for example, the power shower should have plenty of power and if the flooring was described as non-slip that's what it should be.
- Work should be carried out with due care and diligence: for example, tradespeople shouldn't break your things or destroy your property and your coat shouldn't be ruined by the dry cleaner.

The remedies you are entitled to are exactly the same as for goods: repair, replacement or refund (partial or full). Work out what it is that you want to happen and a reasonable remedy for your situation, using the same criteria as described for products earlier in this chapter.

Let's say your car was fixed but exactly the same mechanical problem occurred a couple of weeks later. Whether the cause of this was shoddy workmanship or a defective part, the garage should carry the repair work out again free of charge. Or you could seek a refund from the original garage and pay another garage that you trust to carry out the work.

Or let's imagine that you had patio slabs fitted but the gaps between them were huge or they started cracking after a short time. Repair will be the easiest option for everyone involved but if the result isn't satisfactory, the whole thing will have to be done again, this time properly, or you should get your money back.

Or what if your dentist carried out root canal work and because of that ended up damaging healthy teeth, which then needed treatment. This shouldn't have happened if the dentist carried out the work with the 'necessary skill' and with 'due care and diligence', so he should carry out any extra work needed free of charge, or you go elsewhere for the treatment, and he should cover the cost of the remedial work. Likewise if the dry cleaners ruined your suit, they didn't carry out the service as promised and so should compensate you so that you can replace it.

Think of it like this: your aim is to get back to the beginning, when you had agreed to pay a certain price for a certain service that would turn out a certain way. The service-provider must provide a remedy until this contractual promise is fulfilled.

Yes, any remedy is likely to cost the business, especially in the case of a service, where time is involved. But the company can send defective parts back to the manufacturer for a refund and if they can't carry out the work as promised, they shouldn't be promising it in the first place. That's business!

Tips on Buying Services
When it comes to buying any service, whether the services of an accountant, a solicitor, a doctor or an architect, you should receive exactly what was promised and agreed.

If you don't get what was promised and agreed, a breach of contract has occurred; your consumer rights kick in and I hope you know what to do next – complain and get what you're entitled to.

Below are some tips for avoiding those problems in the first place. For information on what service-providers (and retailers) must adhere to in relation to advertising information and indicating prices, see Chapter 2 on 'Advertising, Price Display and the Hard Sell'.

Price

It is best practice to agree a detailed price up front, where possible. Ask for a detailed written quotation on headed notepaper, with itemised costs for everything, including materials and labour.

When it comes to prices, did you know that solicitors are legally required to issue what's called a Section 68 letter, which should outline their fees or if that isn't possible or practical the basis on which the fee will be calculated. Some merely indicate the hourly rate, resulting in a nasty surprise for clients at the end of the process. Ask your solicitor for a 'meaningful' estimate and for regular updates if necessary so you are aware of the fees they are likely to charge you.

Get a few quotes

Yes, it requires a bit more homework on your part but you should get three quotations if you can so that you can compare value.

Ask neighbours, friends and families for names of businesses they have used as recommendations as this should give you more comfort in who you choose. If you are not familiar with the business you can ask for references, which can be very important, especially if you're paying for expensive work.

When asking for a quotation it's important that you know exactly the work you want done and can be as detailed as possible. Remember that new costs may arise as the job progresses so discuss how this will be handled with the service-provider in advance.

Once you get your quotations take your time to compare and choose and don't let any business put pressure on you for a decision. Having a few quotations will also give you the bargaining tools to engage in some haggling: you'll be much better placed to ask with confidence.

for a reduced price or for something extra to be thrown in.

Know who you're dealing with

This is especially important if you buy a service from someone who calls at the door, offering to fix the roof or pave your driveway. Never do business with someone for whom you don't have full contact details; after all if you only have a mobile number how will you find someone if something goes wrong. And remember just because they're at the door doesn't mean you have to say 'Yes' there and then. Ask for some information, take your time to think the offer over and do some research before you make your mind up.

Buying Services Abroad

At this stage we're all used to buying products in other countries, both online and when we are away on foreign trips. But you can buy services in another country too.

If you live in Ireland it can be pretty easy to head across the border into Northern Ireland to buy services in that jurisdiction. It's not so easy to buy services further afield, despite that fact that we are living in one big European market.

With this in mind, new EU legislation called the Services Directive came into force in November 2010. Its aim is to cut through existing red tape, to make it easier for service-providers to sell in any Member State without having to establish a company in the other country. As a consequence it should be easier for us to buy services elsewhere so we have access to more choice and potentially better deals.

To enable us to find service-providers in other countries, contact points were set up in each country. In Ireland it's the European Consumer Centre (ECC) that can assist with finding a service-provider and provide information on what to check for and on relevant disputes procedures. The centre can also advise if you have a complaint.

Some service-providers are excluded from the scope of this law, including financial, healthcare, transport, audiovisual and gambling services. If you do decide to hire someone from another country, keep in mind the following information that by law the service-provider has to give you:

- The name, legal status and address of the business
- If the business is registered in a trade or other public register, the registered name and the registration number
- Particulars of the regulator if the business is subject to an authorisation scheme in Ireland or another EEA (European
- Economic Area) country
- The relevant ID number if the service is subject to VAT
- If it is a regulated profession, any professional body or similar institution with which the business is registered, the professional title and the EEA country in which that title was granted
- General terms and conditions
- The existence of any contractual terms concerning the competent courts or the law applicable to the contract.
- The existence of any after-sales guarantee (as distinct from legal guarantees)
- The price of the service, where predetermined
- The main features of the service, if not clear from the context
- If the business is required to hold professional liability, insurance or a guarantee, information about the cover and contact details of the insurer and the territorial coverage of the insurance
- The contact details for customers to make a complaint

Businesses Closing Down

This is a sad fact of life, especially at the moment, and you may very well lose out if the retailer or service-provider you bought from goes bust.

If the product becomes faulty and you have no retailer to go back to for a repair, your only hope is to get a remedy from the manufacturer, although you may have to pay for it, especially if you don't have a warranty. If you are seeking a refund or if you have ordered and paid for goods that didn't arrive or a service that wasn't carried out before the business closed down, your situation is not very hopeful. Nonetheless, you should:

- Register as a creditor with whoever is looking after the wind-up of the business. You can check at the Companies' Registration Office (www.cro.ie). Bear in mind that you will be at the bottom of the creditors list, after Revenue and the banks, so it is unlikely you'll get any money back this way.
- If you have paid by credit card or Visa debit card you may be in luck because you can ask your credit provider to provide a charge-back: refund you for items purchased that were not and will not be delivered. Ask your bank about the procedure for applying.
- In general, avoid paying deposits on items with a long delivery date, be careful of buying several months or a year's worth of services up front and use your credit card or Visa debit card to pay – it's the safest method.

Who to Complain To

For information and advice on your rights
- National Consumer Agency (NCA)
  www.consumerconnect.ie/1890-432432/01-4025555
- The Consumers' Association of Ireland (CAI):
  www.thecai.ie/01-4978600
- Citizens Information Service:
  www.citizensnformation.ie/1890-777121/021-4521600

For complaints and disputes relating to cross-border purchase
- European Consumer Centre (ECC) Ireland:
  www.eccireland. ie/01-8797620

For information on finding a service-provider in another Member State
- European Consumer Centre (ECC) Ireland: www.eccireland. ie/01-8797620

If you cannot resolve your complaint against an Irish or EU trader you can have recourse to:
- The small-claims procedure in the district court: www.courts.ie

For complaints relating to:
- Energy supply: Commission for Energy Regulation (CER)/ www.cer.ie
- Telecommunications, premium rate services and postal services: Commission for Communications Regulation (Comreg)/www.comreg.ie
- Architects: Royal Institute of Architects in Ireland/www.riai.ie
- Solicitors: Law Society of Ireland/www.lawsociety.ie
- Doctors: Medical Council/www.medicalcouncil.ie
- Dentists: Dental Council/www.dentalcouncil.ie
- Pharmacists: Pharmaceutical Society of Ireland/ www.thepsi.ie
- Builders: Construction Industry Federation/www.cif.ie
- Electricians: Register of Electrical Contractors of Ireland/ www.reci.ie or Electrical Contractors Safety and Standards Association/www.ecssa.ie
- Auctioneers, Valuers and Surveyors: Society of Chartered Surveyors/www.scsi.ie or Institute of Professional Auctioneers and Valuers/www.ipav.ie

Leglisation Name Check

Sale of Goods and Supply of Services Act 1980.

EC Directive 99/44/EC: Incorporated into Irish law by European Communities (Certain Aspects of the Sale of Consumer Goods and Associated Guarantees) Regulations 2003. Statutory Instrument No 11 of 2003).

Recycling of electrical products

EC Directive 2002/96/EC: Incorporated into Irish law by the Waste Management (Electrical and Electronic Equipment) Regulations 2005. Statutory Instrument No 290 of 2005. As amended by SI No 143 of 2010: Waste Management (Waste Electrical and Electronic Equipment) (Amendment) Regulations 2010.

Services directive

EC Directive 2006/123/EC: Incorporated into Irish law by the European Union (Provision of Services) Regulations 2010. Statutory Instrument No 533 of 2010. Article 42 of the Directive was transposed separately by the European Community's (Court Orders for the Protection of Consumer Interests) Regulations 2010. SI No 555 of 2010.

2

Advertising, Price Displays and the Hard Sell

Advertising and marketing information about the product or service, the price displayed and the selling techniques employed all play a crucial part in your decision-making process about whether to buy any product or service. For this reason there are rules governing all these areas in order to ensure that the business selling to you does not have an unfair advantage.

In other words, no business is allowed to hoodwink you into buying something!

In this Chapter
- Misleading advertising
- Prohibited commercial practices
- General rules on price display
- Specific price display orders
- Who to complain to
- Legislation name check

Misleading Advertising
Under the Consumer Protection Act 2007, it is illegal for an advertiser or business to make false or misleading claims about goods, services or prices.

All types of communications that promote goods or services are covered by the act, including:

- Advertisements
- Notices in shops
- Claims made by a sales assistant about a product or service

The general principles

An advertisement should not contain a false statement or untrue information, misrepresent the price or give a false impression about what the product or service does. So, for example it is wrong if the advertisement includes a picture of a top-of-the-range car but the price is for a basic model. Nor is an advertisement allowed to claim 'free delivery' if there is a charge, or to show a moving toy without telling you that batteries are required.

The National Consumer Agency has drawn up guidelines, which are helpful in understanding how these principles should work:

- Promotional advertising should be 'clear, unambiguous and easily understood'.
- Any relevant information should not be obscured by dis- claimers or provisos in small print.
- Consumers have a right to expect that what they are offered or see is what they get.
- Traders should act with care and diligence and have regard to the principle of 'good faith'.

The idea of 'good faith' may seem a little woolly but it is a term used in the legislation and it means that if the trader cannot show their actions were in 'good faith' (that they weren't trying to con you) they may be in breach of the law and may be prosecuted. This concept of 'good faith' underpins all the rules.

Prohibited Commercial Practices

As well as the provisions against misleading information when selling to consumers, aggressive commercial practices are against the law. An aggressive practice is to engage in harassment or intimidation, for example using threatening or abusive language or behaviour or exploiting a consumer's vulnerability or misfortune.

In addition to aggressive practices, specific practices relating to making false claims are also prohibited by law. Thirty-two practices relating to making false claims are listed. They include: claiming to have the endorsement of a regulatory or approved body; a company declaring they are about to cease trading when they are not; claiming a cure for illness; indicating that a product is free when it costs you more than the reasonable costs to respond to the representation or collect the product or have it delivered; falsely indicating limited availability to encourage quick sales; running promotions or competitions without awarding the prizes described; false invoicing; demanding payment for unsolicited goods.

To put all of this in context these are the types of activity that should not happen:

Sales
The trader should not have an unfair advantage when it comes to pricing the goods, as we're all tempted when we see the sale sign. When something is advertised as being for sale at a sale price, the original price should also be shown. The original price should have been used for a 'reasonable period' prior to the sale. A period of twenty-eight days is recommended, or fourteen days for perishables or seasonal products.

Old stock
It is unlikely that old stock brought out from the storeroom was on sale for twenty-eight days within the previous three months: any old stock should be described as 'old stock' so that you know what you are getting. This is especially important for electrical items that have a limited life span. The same goes for discontinued lines or designer items in an outlet store.

Money off

If the sign says 'up to 70 per cent off', there should be a reasonable amount of stock selling at 70 per cent off. The next question is 70 per cent off what? Again, the original full price should be shown. Likewise if a product has a sign on it saying €50 or 25 per cent off, it is confusing if the discount is included in the price shown. Therefore, both the original and the reduced price should be shown.

Introductory or special offers

These sorts of offers are common practice, especially when a new product is being introduced to the market, but they should come with enough information. 'Special introductory offer of €9.99' is not enough; the sign must indicate when the offer will end and the retail price after the promotion has ended. The special-offer period can be extended but this is allowed only when there is a valid reason.

Signs you should not see
No refunds on sale items

This is illegal as your statutory rights are exactly the same in a sale as they are when you buy at full price. It is okay if the proviso 'this does not affect your statutory rights' is added. That's because the shop is not obliged to refund you for an item you just don't like, they have that obligation only if the item is faulty or not as described. Many shops do alter their returns policy for unwanted goods during sales, so check before you buy.

Closing down sale

This sign is fine if the shop is closing down but the sign should also tell you when the shop is closing. If the business is moving or selling stock, that should also be made clear. A shop cannot 'pretend' to be closing down in order to get you in the door and you have to know the full story so that you don't feel under pressure to buy straight away.

Limited availability

If a product is advertised as having limited availability, the trader must act in 'good faith': this will depend on the facts and the circumstances of the promotion. The item has to have a limited availability in reality and you should be told for how long it will be available. If the offer is a ploy to encourage you to make hasty or unplanned decisions, it is a misleading action. Such actions are prohibited.

Bait advertising

A car-dealer advertises cars for sale: 'This year's model – only €3000'. But the dealer has no intention of selling the cars at this price. He merely used this type of advertising to encourage consumers to visit his showroom in the hope of increasing business. This is an example of bait advertising, which is prohibited.

Also prohibited are 'bait and switch' tactics. This is when an item is offered for sale at a very attractive price when the trader has no intention of selling the advertised product or is not in a position to provide it. The purpose of the 'bait' is to entice customers into the store and once this objective is achieved, customers are advised that the product is no longer in stock and actively encouraged to purchase a different product.

For example a trader advertises a 32-inch television for €300. When the customer asks about it he shows him a set with a 'sold' tag. He explains that all the other sets have been sold and the only one left is 'faulty'. He then refers the customer to an alternative model of television, which he claims is superior, although it may cost more. If the trader intentionally uses this practice to promote a different make or model, this would be regarded as 'bait and switch 'and would be in breach of the act.

The National Consumer Agency (NCA) has an arsenal of powers to deal with misleading or aggressive practices: prosecution; issuing of compliance notices; ordering written undertakings; issuing prohibition orders; and fixed payment notices with fines. The NCA publishes regular lists of actions taken, along with the details of the offending businesses. Read them on www. consumerconnect.ie.

Price matching

If a store promises they will match a price if a customer finds a lower one in another store, they have to tell you any terms: only on certain products, for a certain period and so on. If they claim they have the 'lowest price to be found', this has to be backed up by evidence.

Free offers

A newspaper or magazine advertises 'Free DVD' on the front cover. However, when the consumer buys the publication he finds out that it is necessary to collect a number of tokens to claim the DVD. In effect this means that the consumer will have to incur the cost of purchasing a number of publications to claim the 'free offer', so it isn't really free! Instead traders should make it clear to consumers exactly what is involved in getting the 'free' or 'reduced price' offer at the time the offer is made. For example the advertisement should say that you have to collect five tokens, with one available in each day's paper, so that you know the outlay involved in getting the free DVD.

If there are any other payments to be made in order to avail of the offer, for example postal charges or a premium-rate call, these should also be indicated. Traders should not claim that an offer is free if they try to offset the cost of the 'free' offer by imposing additional charges that wouldn't normally apply, such as inflating the price of postage or using premium telephone charges.

General Rules on Price Display

In relation to price we need to know how much we are paying for goods so the price needs to be clearly displayed. This is crucial so we can easily compare prices between different brands on offer and between shops.

Goods
- Price legislation covers goods sold in shops and also by mail order, catalogue and online. In these cases the price should always be displayed.
- The price should be displayed on the product or near it, for example on the edge of the display shelf.
- Prices must be shown in euro but there is no rule to say that other currencies can't be shown also, or indeed that the euro price has to appear more prominent.

The final price
- The price shown should be the final price: that is, it should include VAT and any other taxes and charges.
- There are exceptions to this rule: for goods sold at auction, provided in the course of a service or sold in bulk when the final selling price is set only when the consumer has decided how much/many to buy.
- On some invoices, for example phone and electricity bills, VAT can be shown separately. The same goes for business-to-business sales.

Unit sales
When it comes to goods sold by weight or volume, the price also has to show the unit price, so that's why you see the 'per kilo' price on food products in the supermarket. This is really important as it allows us to compare the actual price by weight, given that so many similar food products are sold in quantities with a different weight.

Is the price I see the price I pay?
Yes it should be. So if you see a jar of pasta sauce priced at €1 but then go to the till and it is scanned at €1.50, you should not have to pay the higher price. Complain to the store manager and the

National Consumer Agency, which regularly issues compliance notices to stores for such behaviour.

On the other hand, let's say you are in a clothes shop and all the trousers on a rail are marked at €50 apart from one pair, which is marked at €35. In that case you are not necessarily entitled to buy it for the lower price, assuming that this is a genuine mistake on the shop's part.

The deal is sealed only when your offer to buy the trousers at €35 is accepted: the shop can decline your offer, saying it was a mistake. Let's say, however, that the whole rail of trousers is priced at €35 and when you go to the till the salesperson tells you they are all in fact €50. In that case, you may have deliberately been misled on the price. This is not allowed and you should be able to buy the product for the price displayed.

Price fixing
If prices are being kept high deliberately by a monopoly of one big company or by a cartel of a number of businesses, this could be price-fixing, which against competition rules. If you suspect price-fixing, report it to the Competition Authority:www.tca. ie/01-804 5400.

Services
The rules are different when it comes to services. For example, the end price may depend on what you request from the service-provider. Nevertheless, the service-provider must inform you of the total cost of the service and how the price was calculated before you seal the deal.

In certain advertisements for concerts and theatre performances it is permissible to show ticket prices and booking fees separately but the reason for this must be stated: for example, the advertiser may specify an additional booking charge or administration fee. There are specific rules on the display of airfares. See Chapter 11 for details.

Specific Price Display Orders

There are specific price display orders that relate to how certain sectors must display their prices. This is so that we can compare prices easily before committing to buying.

Hairdressers and barbers

- They have to display an up-to-date price list for each service provided.
- The list must be visible either from the street or immediately inside the entrance to the premises.

Petrol stations

- Prices have to be displayed by the litre for petrol and diesel.
- The sign showing prices has to be clearly visible from the side of the road.
- The writing on the sign has to be at least 20cm in height.
- Needless to say the price displayed has to match the price at the pump.

Pubs and other licensed premises (excluding off-licences)

- Outside or just inside the premises there must be a price display. It has to be a list of prices of sixteen specific drinks.
- There must also be a display of drink prices within each drinking area.

Restaurants, cafes, hotels and pubs serving food

- Prices must be displayed outside the premises and on the menus or on something like a blackboard if there are no individual menus. The price list should also show a minimum charge, the service charge and any cover charge.
- If different prices are charged at different times, these should also be shown.

Doctors and dentists

There is no specific law requiring either doctors or dentists to display their fees. However, in February 2011 the Dental Council of Ireland approved a code of practice relating to the display of private fees in dental practices. The code took effect in June 2011 and should be followed by the council's registered members. This means that you should be able to view the prices charged before you go in for treatment.

The Dental Council of Ireland code stipulates the following:
- The fees notice should be at least A4 in size and be legible, accurate and up-to-date.
- It must be prominently displayed in the practice, where patients can see it before the consultation.
- Recommended places for the notice are: the entrance to the practice, the reception area and the waiting room.
- A minimum list of treatments for which fees must be displayed are set out; some treatments require a single fee (extractions, for example) and for others (for example, crowns) there should be a minimum and maximum fee.
- Fees should be transparent and inclusive of all costs.

Pyramid Selling

Remember those get-rich-quick schemes where you 'invested' money and got a big payback for doing nothing but recommending the scheme to others? These are pyramid schemes and they are banned.

In fact, organising, promoting and even participating in such a scheme is prohibited.

If you're involved in a pyramid scheme both the National Consumer Agency and the Gardaí have powers to take action and if convicted you face a fine of up to €150,000 or imprisonment for up to five years or both.

Who to Complain To

If prices are not displayed or if displayed prices don't match the price at the till or if you believe an advertisement is misleading or a business is engaging in an 'unfair commercial practice' you should bring it to the attention of the National Consumer Agency (NCA)/ www.consumerconnect.ie/1890 432432/01-4025555.

If you believe an advertisement is offensive or has questionable standards: The Advertising Standards Authority (ASAI)/www.asai. ie/01-6608766.

If you believe that a business is engaging in uncompetitive behaviour, such as price fixing: The Competition Authority/www. tca.ie/01-804 5400.

Legislation Name Check

Misleading advertising, information and aggressive commercial practices
Directive 2005/29/EC on unfair business-to-consumer commercial practices in the internal market was transposed into Irish law by the Consumer Protection Act 2007 (No 19 of 2007).

Directive 2006/114/EC incorporated into Irish law by EC (misleading and comparative marketing communications) Regulations 2007. Statutory Instrument No 774 of 2007.

Price display
Directive 98/6/EC incorporated into Irish law by EC (Requirements to Indicate Product Prices) Regulations 2002. Statutory Instrument No 639 of 2002.

Price display orders
Statutory Instrument No 156 of 1976: Charges (hairdressing) Display Order 1976.

Statutory Instrument No 178 of 1997: Retail Prices (diesel and petrol) Display Order 1997.

Statutory Instrument No 263 of 1999: Retail Prices (beverages in licensed premises) Display Order 1999.

Statutory Instrument No 213 of 1984: Retail Prices (food in catering establishments) Display Order 1984.

Statutory Instrument No 103 of 1997: Consumer Information (advertisements for concerts or theatre performances) Order 1997.

Statutory Instrument No 468 of 2000: Consumer Information (advertisements for airfares) Order 2000.

3

Shopping Online

You might love the hustle and bustle of the high street but sitting on your sofa browsing the internet for products, comparing prices and buying, all while still in your pyjamas, is the modern way to shop and can be very handy indeed.

The biggest differences are that you may not know the business you are buying from, you are not talking to a salesperson and getting their measure and the business you are dealing with may be based in another country.

This is precisely why there is a separate set of consumer rights when it comes to shopping online. In order to shop safely online you need to know what they are.

In this Chapter
- Your rights when you shop online
- How to avoid fraudulent sites
- Internet auctions: tips on safe buying
- Internet auctions: tips on safe selling
- VAT/customs implications when buying online
- Frustrations in the online marketplace
- Focus: buying tickets online
- Who to complain to
- Legislation name check

Your Rights when You Shop Online

When you shop online the good news is that you have additional rights that don't exist when you shop on the high street.

Remember these rights are for shopping within the EU only. If you are buying outside the EU, make sure to read all the terms and conditions very carefully. These rights do not cover all types of online shopping; let's start with these:

- Internet auctions
- Goods made to your specification or personalised
- Audio, video or software products of which you have removed the seal
- Newspapers, periodicals and magazines
- Gaming and lottery services
- Services where the service has already begun before the end of the seven-day cooling-off period
- The supply of goods or services, the price of which is dependent on fluctuations in the financial market which cannot be controlled by the supplier
- Plane, train or concert tickets or hotel bookings: cases in which the supply of services is for a specific time or date
- Food and drink delivered to your home or at work by regular roundsmen: for example, milkmen, supermarket delivery
- Financial services
- Contracts for the sale of land
- Purchases from an individual, as such purchases are not considered consumer contracts

Faulty products

To start with you have the same rights as when you shop on the high street. That is to say that if a product is faulty or not 'as described' you are entitled to a repair, replacement or refund.

If you have to return a faulty product you should not have to pay the cost of return postage. In practice what usually happens is that you pay to post the faulty item back and this postage cost is refunded to you.

A good idea is to check the item immediately on delivery to make sure it is what you ordered and not in several hundred broken pieces. When it comes to consumer problems, always act as promptly as you can.

Information

By law a web trader must include the following information on their site:

- Name and address
- The main characteristics of the good/service
- The price, including taxes and delivery costs, and how payment is to be made
- How the goods are to be delivered or how the service will be performed
- That a right to cancel exists
- The minimum duration of the contract
- How long it will be open to you to enter into the contract on these terms
- The cost of the communication between the parties if it is above a basic rate
- How to cancel the contract
- Any guarantees and after-sales services that are available

These details must be provided to you by email or in writing before or at the time of delivery. Before choosing to buy, check that all this information is there and if it isn't, don't buy from that site.

Think about it. If all you have is an email address for the company, what will happen if you need to contact them later and they don't respond? How do you even know which country they are based in? If the business can't be bothered to comply with the law on this, can you rely on them?

Cooling-off period

This is the biggie, something you don't get when shopping at your bricks-and-mortar retailer.

The cooling-off period means that you have a legal entitlement to change your mind about whatever it is you bought and return it. You have seven days from the day you receive the goods or if it's a service, from the day the contract was concluded or the day you receive the delivery details, whichever is later.

If you decide you don't want the product or service, tell the web trader within seven days. You are not even obliged to give a reason (although the trader may ask for feedback for business reasons).

By the way, that 'cooling-off' period extends to three months if all the required information, as stated above, is not provided.

Non-delivery

It's pretty obvious that if you never receive the item you bought, the trader should either get busy delivering or give you a refund. You have the law on your side here too. The legislation states that the contract must be performed within thirty days of the order being placed, unless you have agreed otherwise with the trader. Otherwise you are entitled to cancel the contract and get a refund.

In such situations it can happen that the trader blames the courier or delivery company for non-delivery and asks you to complain to them. Don't do this. The trader is trying to fob you off: he is responsible for getting the product to you.

The same rules that protect you when you are shopping online govern other distance sales, like buying from a catalogue or over the phone.

New rules from 2013

In October 2011 the EU Council of Ministers formally adopted a new EU Consumer Rights Directive, which updates the current distance-selling rules. This new law is due to be in force across the EU before the end of 2013. The main changes will be:

1. The total price, including any extras, has to be shown before you place an order. If not, you won't have to pay any extras.
2. The cooling-off period will extend to fourteen days.
3. The cooling-off period will extend to one year if the trader has not informed you of it.
4. The cooling-off period will begin once you receive the goods rather than when the contract is concluded.
5. The trader will have to refund you within fourteen days of your withdrawal and cover delivery costs.
6. If you have to pay for delivery of goods returned within the cooling-off rules, the trader must inform you of this in advance. Otherwise they have to pay for return delivery costs.
7. The cooling-off period or right of withdrawal will extend to internet auctions but only when you've purchased from a professional seller.
8. Traders will not be able to charge consumers more for paying by credit card (or other means of payment) than what it actually costs them to offer such means of payment. In other words, no surcharges on card payments will be allowed.
9. Pre-ticked boxes will be banned. In other words, you'll always have to opt in to something rather than un-tick a box to opt-out.

'Deal of the day' sites

Thousands of us have embraced the opportunity to buy products and services at discounted rates, through dozens of websites in Ireland that offer heavily discounted deals of the day.

Most of the deals are lifestyle-related, such as beauty treatments, hotel stays and activities, although more practical offers are on the increase. Discounts can be as much as 80 per cent.

Be clever about it, though! You may be getting a discount but it's not a good deal if you never use it or didn't really want it or need it in the first place. All deals purchased come with a limited lifetime so make sure you use the deal soon after purchase to make sure that you get the booking you want and that you don't forget you have it.

Given that you are purchasing the voucher online, you are entitled to your seven-day cooling-off period: you can inform the seller (in this case, the 'deal' site) that you are cancelling and get a refund. This should be detailed in the terms and conditions on the website.

How to Avoid Fraudulent Sites

It can happen that you end up finding a great deal online and unwittingly pay a fraudster who never had any intention of delivering anything to you.

The best way to avoid getting conned by con artists is to do your research carefully:

- Shop with a known and reputable trader if you can.
- If you are unsure about the site do a search on the company and see if you can find any negative chat online. Many people tend to carry out this search after something has gone wrong, then find the bad news and wish they had checked before purchase. You can avoid making this mistake.
- Make sure you have full contact details for the trader (i.e. address and telephone number) and not just the website address or an email address.
- Read the terms and conditions of the sale.
- Check that the web trader has included information on delivery, cancellation, returns, complaints, data protection and security on the site and read this information.

- Find out if there is a choice of payment method.
- Make sure you know what the full price is, in euro and including tax and delivery charges, to avoid any surprises when you get your credit card statement.

Internet Auctions: Tips for Safe Buying

Shopping on internet auction sites is currently excluded from the provisions of the distance-selling legislation so you should vigilantly follow the safety tips of the auction site you are using, whether buying or selling.

Know your seller

Once you have found an item you want to bid on, get to know the seller. You can do this by checking the seller's rating and reading all the feedback about them. You should also ask the seller questions about the item and make sure your questions have been answered before committing to buying.

Know the item

Make sure you know what you are buying. Look at the photo and ask for more photos – maybe of the soles of a shoe or the stitching on a bag. Compare the price with that of similar items: be aware that if a designer bag is selling for €50 it may be a fake. Ask if there is a returns policy (there may not be), what the postage costs are and how long delivery will take.

Safe payments

Ask the seller what payment methods are accepted and follow the payment guidelines of the auction site. If the seller asks you to conclude the transaction off-site do not do it as you will then be outside the protection of the site. If the seller asks you to pay via money transfer don't do that either as you cannot trace where the money has gone.

- Always check that the web trader has a secure payment mechanism. Just before a purchase is made the retailer's address should change from 'http' to 'https', the 's' standing for a secure connection and safety.

- In addition, look for the padlock symbol on the bottom right corner of the web page. This is a security icon and you can click on it to ensure that the retailer has an encryption certificate, which helps to ensure that your personal information will be sent safely.

- Be alert for traders who offer you a choice of payment method between credit card and money or bank transfer. The sting is that they charge an exorbitant premium (as much as 20 per cent) for credit card payments to encourage you to pay by money transfer instead. That means that you don't have the protection that comes from paying with your credit card. These traders are bad news.

- Paying by credit card or Visa debit card is the safest: if the trader goes bust, disappears, or if there is a problem that you cannot resolve with them, you can contact your credit provider and request a chargeback for the amount paid.

Disputes

If you have a complaint you should first address it to the seller to try to resolve it. If this doesn't work use the dispute resolution mechanisms provided by the site itself. Read the rules carefully, as you usually need to use this facility within a limited period. For example on eBay you have to open the dispute with forty-five days and if there is no satisfactory response from the seller you must escalate the dispute and look for a refund within twenty days.

Internet Auctions: Tips for Safe Selling
Know your buyer
You will have given detailed information on the item you are selling, its price and delivery options and charges but it is no harm to chat a bit to the buyer to make sure they are legitimate. Also check any buyer feedback available.

Accepting payments

Read the auction site's advice on accepting payments carefully and complete every transaction on site. Tell your customer what payments you will accept and send an invoice promptly. If you decide to accept cheques or postal orders, make sure you allow them to clear before dispatching the item. Remember that just because you have lodged the cheque to your account this doesn't mean the money is there; it can take up to a week for a cheque to clear. Do not accept money transfers. Do not accept 'overpayments'. This is where someone offers a cheque for a greater amount and asks you to return the difference, usually via money transfer. Inevitably, the buyer's cheque will bounce and you will have sent the product and the extra sum.

VAT and Customs Implications when Buying Online
VAT

When you buy online in the EU, the trader will charge you Ireland's VAT rate as they will be registered for payment of VAT here unless their revenue is below €35,000 per annum. So don't think you can automatically pay the lower German VAT rate of 19 per cent rather than the 21 per cent current in Ireland. The reduced rate is 13.5 per cent and there is no VAT on children's clothes or on books.

Bear this in mind if you are checking the advertised prices on European sites as the VAT element may become clear only when you go to the checkout and enter your country of residence. It may be a welcome surprise if you are shopping on Danish or Swedish sites as the VAT rate in these countries is 25 per cent but the opposite if you're shopping on a Spanish site as their VAT rate is currently 18 per cent. If you are buying from outside the EU, from a US website for example, you will also pay the Irish VAT rate. The goods are VAT-exempt, however, if the value is less than €22 and gifts are VAT exempt up to €45 (the value has to be declared). If VAT is payable it will be added to the new total, after customs duty has been levied.

Customs

There are no customs charges within the EU but if you buy from a non-EU website, say one in the US, you will have to pay customs duty on purchases.

You are allowed to buy €150 worth of goods online free of customs charges. Once you reach this threshold customs duty is added (on the purchase price plus postage costs) at different rates: for example, 2.7 per cent or 3.7 per cent for toys, 12 per cent for clothes, 17 per cent for shoes. Then VAT at 21.5 per cent (2011 rate) is added to the new total.

This also applies to gifts. Some big web traders will factor the customs cost in when you are at the checkout but others simply advise you that you will have to pay VAT and customs charges in your own country so take out your calculator before you decide if it is really the best deal.

Bear in mind that if you haven't paid the customs duty at the till the goods will not be delivered to you until you pay up but you may not realise this until you get a knock on the door from a delivery man asking for more money.

For further information on VAT and customs charges on imports go to www.revenue.ie.

Frustrations in the online marketplace

The growth of the virtual marketplace means that in theory we have access to an enormous choice of products from around the world at the click of a mouse and can get what we want at the best price available.

In practice it isn't always so simple. In fact, in the EU 40 per cent of people shop online in their own countries but only 23 per cent do so beyond their national borders. However the Irish do buck the trend with a greater number (34 per cent) shopping online in another country compared to those shopping online with a home trader (26 per cent).*

Trust as well as access is still important, as consumers are more likely to trust online traders in their own country or that of a near neighbours.

In addition, even within the EU, despite there being no economic borders, there are separate regulatory environments, different VAT rules, differences in consumer rights and variations in language and marketing. As it is up to any trader to choose to whom they wish to sell, traders may choose not to sell to a particular market, including Ireland.

*(Source: European Parliament, *Consumer Behaviour in a Digital Environment*, 2011)

Focus: Buying Tickets Online

Your heart might lead your head if you are desperate to see your favourite football team play or your music hero perform. It is precisely for this reason that you become vulnerable to buying overpriced tickets from dodgy sellers.

Essentially, the only way you can be 100 per cent sure that you will: a) pay face value; b) get the ticket; and c) gain entry, is by buying from the official or authorised ticket agent.

In Ireland it is not illegal to sell on tickets. But for many events the terms and conditions of the ticket will stipulate that they cannot be sold on and that doing so will breach the contract of sale. But this doesn't stop pretty much any ticket for any event being available somewhere online.

Online ticket touts operate in a number of ways. Either they buy loads of tickets when they go on sale, or if the number of ticket purchases allowed is limited they hire people to each buy as may as they can, then they advertise them for sale at an inflated price. Other touts engage in 'speculative selling'; that is they take your order and cash and then they try to source a ticket for you. Or they may be agents who will take your cash and hook you up with a tout who will later provide the ticket.

Then there are the out-and-out fraudsters. These people set up sites, usually for a specific event or tour, but they never have tickets and their intention was only ever to get your money.

Whether you buy from an online tout or from an individual selling on a ticket, be careful, do your research, read the terms and conditions and think twice – things can go wrong:

- You may not receive the ticket.
- You will pay above face value for it.
- You may receive a ticket but not, as promised, for the side of the stadium where the supporters of your team sit.
- Refunds for undelivered tickets may be promised but not be forthcoming.
- The total price you pay may include hefty administration and delivery fees on top of the ticket price so if you do get a refund, you may not be refunded these additional charges.
- You may be refused entry to the event. Remember that organisers can cancel tickets if their terms and conditions don't allow onward selling and they spot one for sale online. If the ticket is ID-linked you probably won't gain entry either.

Or your ticket could be bogus.

- Knowing that all this could happen, the best you can do, if you must buy from a secondary source, is to carry out a lot of research. But even then, think twice.

Money-saving tip

If you are buying online you may as well do it via a cashback website. These websites link you up with hundreds of well-known traders. You click on your web trader of choice and peruse and purchase online as normal. But cookies on your computer trace you as having come from the cashback site and thanks to agreements in place between the traders and these sites, they will give you back money.

This is money for nothing. It might be 5 per cent or 10 per cent of the purchase price or a flat amount. Either way the cashback site pays it into your PayPal or bank account and then it is your money to spend as you please.

The cashback sites currently operating in Ireland are:
- www.bethrifty.ie
- www.fatcheese.ie
- www.cashbackireland.com

Who to Complain To

- As with any purchase, complain directly to the trader first and try to resolve things that way.
- If this doesn't work you can take small claims action for up to €2000 against an Irish or EU trader at a cost of €18: www.courts.ie.
- Contact the National Consumer Agency for advice on your online shopping rights: www.consumerconnect.ie/ 1890-432432/01-4055555 or the Consumers' Association of Ireland: www.thecai.ie/01-4978600.

- If your complaint is about a trader based in another EU country contact the European Consumer Centre for their assistance in resolving your dispute: www.eccireland.ie/01-8797620.

Legislation Name Check

Distance selling

Directive 97/7/EC transposed in Ireland as EC Protection of consumers in respect of contracts made by means of distance communications Regulations 2001. Statutory Instrument No 207 of 2001 and amended by SI No 370 of 2010.

4

Shopping and Telephoning Abroad

We travel so much these days it's inevitable that we end up buying something when we are away. Whether it's some new clothes or a camera or you end up buying into a timeshare or holiday club, you should be aware of your rights and the potential pitfalls.

In addition, most of us can't be parted from our mobile phones. In the past, many consumers suffered bill shock after returning from abroad. You need to know the rules that are in place governing roaming so that you can choose how to use your phone while abroad.

In this Chapter
- Your consumer rights in the EU
- Bringing goods in from further afield
- Tobacco and alcohol: inside the EU
- Tobacco and alcohol: outside the EU
- Focus: electronics
- Focus: jewellery
- Focus: counterfeit
- Focus: timeshares and holiday clubs
- Mobile roaming
- Who to complain to
- Legislation name check

Your Consumer Rights in the EU
Being EU citizens means we can move freely throughout EU

countries and bring whatever we buy back home without a problem and without any customs or excise requirements. More good news is that there is a minimum standard of consumer protection across the Member States. This means that whichever country you shop in you can always be confident that you have entitlements.

When you shop anywhere in the EU your rights are pretty much the same as they are when shopping in Ireland (see Chapter 1 on goods and services) so you can shop secure in the knowledge that it is no riskier than buying on your local high street.

The product has to conform to the description given and do what it is supposed to do. If not you are entitled to a remedy: a repair, replacement or a partial or full refund.

The one big difference is the time limit for making a claim. Under European legislation that time limit is two years so this is the minimum time limit that can apply in any Member State. European rules provide a minimum standard and Member States are free to impose stricter rules. For example, in Ireland we have a six-years time limit for taking claims and in the UK it's also six but Scotland has a five-year time limit.

Note: if you are coming from the Canary Islands, Gibraltar or the Channel Islands you may have to pay customs charges. This is because, while they are part of the customs territory of the EU, they are outside the EU fiscal territory.

Bringing Goods In from Further Afield
Once you travel outside the EU you are leaving behind the minimum standards of consumer protection that you enjoy across the European bloc. Of course there will be consumer protection rules in the country you are visiting but they will be different from European and Irish rules. Your best bet is to ask in-store what will happen if something goes wrong, especially if you are buying a high-ticket item.

The other difference is that when you buy outside the EU, the goods you bring into Ireland may be subject to customs duty, excise duty and VAT.

Duty and VAT

When applicable, customs duty, excise duty and VAT are payable at the airport or seaport on your arrival back into Ireland from a non-EU country.

What you have to pay will depend on the type of goods you have purchased and their value. If you are travelling in a group you are not allowed to share goods among the members in order to pool individual allowances and if you are under seventeen you cannot bring in tobacco or alcohol.

For personal use or as a gift (i.e. not for sale or commercial use), you are allowed to bring into Ireland goods to the value of €430 (or €215 for under-fifteens) before duty applies. After that, there is a standard duty rate of 2.5 per cent for goods worth up to €700. Above that value various percentages apply, for example 12 per cent on most clothes.

Once the customs duty is added on, VAT is calculated on the new total, either at the standard 21 per cent or at a lower or zero rate if that applies. For example zero per cent VAT is charged on children's clothes and books.

Example

You arrive in Ireland from the US. You are bringing with you a new dress that cost €300, a digital camera worth €600 and several tops with a total value of €500. The dress costs less than €430 so it is allowed under your allowance. No duty is charged on the camera and the value of the tops is less than €700 so a standard 2.5 per cent applies. The total customs duty is €12.50 (€700 x 2.5 per cent).

Then VAT has to be added. Again the dress is allowed but VAT is applied at 21 per cent on €1312.50, which is the total value of the camera (€600) plus tops (€712.50). The VAT comes to €275.63. The total you pay is €12.50 customs duty plus €275.63 VAT, which amounts to €288.13.

Tobacco and Alcohol: inside the EU

If you are coming from another EU country you won't have to pay duty on cigarettes and alcohol. But they must be for personal use and you must carry them: that is, you can't sell them on, nor can you ship them separately.

While there are no strict legal limits there are guidelines as to the quantities that are considered reasonable for personal use:

Tobacco
- 800 cigarettes
- 400 cigarillo
- 200 cigars
- 1kg tobacco

Alcohol
- 10 litres spirits
- 20 litres port, sherry, liqueurs not exceeding 22 per cent by volume
- 90 litres wine
- 110 litres beer

Tobacco and Alcohol: outside the EU

If you're arriving from outside the EU you can legally bring in certain quantities of tobacco products or alcohol without incurring any additional charges but if you go over these strict limits you will be charged customs, excise and VAT. And remember, these must be for personal use only, or intended as a gift.

Tobacco

- 200 cigarettes
- 100 cigarillos
- 50 cigars
- 250 grams tobacco

Alcohol

- 1 litre spirits
- 2 litres port, sherry, sparkling wine and liqueurs not exceeding 22 per cent by volume
- 4 litres wine
- 16 litres beer

Focus: Electronics

Your holiday in the sun can be a perfect chance to snap up a bargain digital camera or camcorder but complaints made to the European Consumer Centre network show that many people have been misled about cameras purchased. There have been many complaints relating to purchases made in the Canary Islands in particular.

Typical problems

- You buy a camera under the impression that it is a well-known make, only to find out that it has a similar name but is not the big brand you thought it was but a 'look alike'.
- The salesperson shows and describes one type of camera but a different and inferior model ends up in the box.
- The salesperson tells you that the expensive camera you are buying is selling at a knock-down price and comes with all the bells and whistles. Instead it is overpriced and doesn't come

with all the functions described to you. At the end of the day you could end up paying more than €1000 for something worth €100.

The common denominator in these scenarios is the hard sell. If you express interest in a particular model sales assistants will sometimes direct you to another, saying that it is a top-of-the-range model and at a much better price that you would pay at home. They reassure you about the quality of the product, often keeping you in the shop for a long while and maybe adding extras as a sweetener.

Once you have purchased the camera and realise something is amiss, it can be very difficult to get a remedy as you'll have to prove that a misleading description was given to you in the shop. Here are some tips to prevent this happening in the first place.

- Before you buy do some research on the type of camera and the functions you want.
- If you feel the shop assistant is pressurising you into buying something you're unsure about, walk away.
- Take your time. If the seller claims the offer is only for that day, be very wary.
- If you are interested in the offer, take a note of the make and model on offer and go online to discover whether or not it's a worthwhile purchase.
- If you do buy, make sure you get the name and address of the shop so you can locate it later if you have a complaint.

Focus: Jewellery

A lot of people buy rings, especially engagement rings, when on holiday abroad. Unfortunately it can happen that when the ring is valued on their return home, the value turns out to be less than they were led to believe. Here are some tips to prevent this happening:

- If you are buying an engagement ring make sure the answer will be 'Yes!' And check the returns policy of the jeweller before taking the leap.
- Buy from a reputable jeweller who is a member of a national association in that country.
- Look for a hallmark where possible. Although it is not compulsory, it is a guarantee of the quality of the metal used in the ring: for example, whether it is 18-carat or 22-carat gold.
- Insist on a certificate for the stones you are buying in the piece. In the case of diamonds, you should ensure that the colour of the stone, the cut, carat, cost, dimensions and weight of the ring are all documented on headed notepaper. If the jeweller is unwilling to provide this information, walk away.

Focus: Counterfeit

There is a host of reasons why buying counterfeit products either at home or abroad is never a good idea:

1. You are damaging the legitimate economy as the trade in counterfeit goods affects industry's earnings and as a consequence taxes collected and potential jobs.
2. You are supporting criminal activity. Many counterfeit gangs are fronts for activities such as drug smuggling and prostitution.
3. There are also potential health risks if you buy electrical products, toys, personal-care items and cigarettes. They are not going to comply with product safety rules and you have no idea where or how they are made and whether parts or ingredients are safe.
4. You will have no comeback if something goes wrong.
5. According to the World Health Organisation as much as 8-10 per cent of medicines in the global supply chain is counterfeit. When it comes to medicines sold online a majority is fake or substandard. In fact in Ireland it is illegal to supply prescription-only medicinal products online. If you do buy them you have no idea what you are getting: the medicine might contain no active ingredients so while it may be harmless it will not do your

condition any good. Or it could have harmful ingredients. Get medical advice instead.

Focus: Timeshare and Holiday Clubs

Problems with timeshare and holiday clubs were very common in the past as tourists became victims of aggressive selling techniques and were mis-sold products for thousands of euro. A timeshare agreement means that you sign up to spend a specified amount of time each year in particular holiday accommodation. A holiday club means that you pay to become a member of a club that promises to offer luxury holidays at knock-down prices.

What could happen:

- Someone approaches you on the street or the beach and gives you a scratch card. You inevitably win something and are then invited to attend a presentation to collect your prize. The prize generally doesn't materialise but the presentation turns into a hard sell for you to sign up to a holiday scheme.
- Consumers have been known to feel trapped and even bullied into handing over credit card details, just to leave the presentation.
- With holidays clubs consumers have discovered that sometimes the holidays don't exist or could be found more cheaply on the high street. Or else the company disappears.
- You own a timeshare and are approached by a resale company offering to sell on your timeshare. You pay an up-front administration fee and the company disappears.

Your rights

In the past legislation covered only timeshare agreements. Thankfully, in February 2011, new legislation came into force which gives consumers additional protection if they sign up either to timeshare or holiday clubs. It also covers resale companies that offer to sell timeshares, as there have been significant problems with bogus resale companies and also with exchange clubs, through which timeshare owners can exchange their week with other timeshare owners. The legislation now covers 'moveable' properties – that is canal boats, caravans or cruise ships, which were excluded before this.

- The most important thing you need to know is that you have a 'cooling-off' period of fourteen days when you can change your mind and withdraw from the contract.
- There is a ban on taking deposits within the cooling-off period, including advance payments.
- If you sign up to a holiday club the entire amount payable for membership cannot be paid up-front. Instead you can pay in equal yearly instalments and will have the opportunity to withdraw from the contract each year.
- Contracts of less than three years are covered by the rules (previously they weren't).
- A huge amount of clear and transparent information must be provided to you before you sign any contract, including: the seller's details; the price and other charges; a description of the property and its location; the provision of services; maintenance and repair; your right to cancel the contract and how you can do this.
- You are entitled to a copy of the contract in English.

Mobile Roaming

The EU roaming regulation came into force at the end of August 2007 and capped the charges for making and receiving calls abroad. Roaming charges are higher than local charges because you're being charged by your home operator, who is also passing on a charge the foreign operator with whom you are roaming has imposed on them.

Price control is uncommon. The European Commission had put pressure on the telecoms providers to reduce roaming charges but felt that they were still too high, so it decided legally to impose price caps.

The current capped roaming charges
- Wholesale download charges between operators are capped at 50c.
- Charges for making and receiving a call are capped at 35c and 11c respectively (ex VAT).
- Charges for texts are capped at 11c (ex VAT).
- Operators must employ per-second billing after thirty seconds when you make a call and from the first second when you receive a call.
- There is a cut-off maximum of €50 for data downloads although you can negotiate a higher cut-off point with your provider if you want.
- Once you have used 80 per cent of your download limit your provider has to send you a warning message. If you continue to download, once you reach your limit you should receive information about how to keep on downloading data or else be cut off.

Don't forget Skype for free Skype-to-Skype calls or very cheap calls from Skype to landlines or mobile phones anywhere in the world. Skype is normally used via your computer but you can get Skype-enabled packages for your phone or download the Skype app to your Smartphone.

Other apps that are useful for your Smartphone include Viber, which gives you free calls anywhere once you and the person you are calling have downloaded the app, and WhatsApp, which gives you free messaging when both users have the app.

Like Skype, these apps use your internet connection so if you are using them on your phone while abroad, use only when you are in a free wifi area or if your provider is offering free data roaming abroad. Otherwise you would be better off disabling your internet connection to avoid paying often very high download fees while abroad.

The regulation was initially to last two years but it has been renewed and extended since then. Caps on texting charges and new data download rules were also introduced. These caps will remain in force until 30 June 2012 and may be extended again.

Other things you need to know:

- Your mobile operator may provide roaming packages with better prices.
- If you miss a call or your phone is turned off you cannot be charged for voicemail. But there still may be a charge via the host operator for relaying the call in the first instance.
- There are several mobile networks in each country. When you arrive at your destination, you will probably be automatically connected to one network but this may not necessarily be the cheapest one for you. Before your trip, check with your mobile provider to see if there is a particular network you should select in the country you are visiting.

This story won't end when current caps expire on 30 June 2012! The European Commission is still monitoring the development of the roaming market and prices charged in order to ensure decent competition. In July 2011 the Commission announced that phone companies still make 'outrageous profits' on roaming services so capping charges continued after this date, with the maximum allowed charges decreasing further.

The Commission has proposed that by 1 July 2014, roaming customers would pay no more than 24c to make a call, 10c to receive a call, 10c to send a text and 50c per mb to download data.

In addition they propose that from 2014 consumers would have an option to buy a roaming package separately from their national package. It should be possible to buy it from any provider in order to avail of the best deals and the customer will be able to keep their own number.

The Commission also proposes that mobile operators would have the right to use the networks of other operators in other Member States at regulated wholesale prices, to encourage more competition.

The Commission believes that by continuing to impose these regulations on mobile operators, they will bring about sufficient competition in the roaming marketplace. To make sure of this, they are even proposing to retain caps on wholesale charges between operators until 2022.

The immediate goal is to ensure that by 2015 the difference between national and roaming costs will be zero. Fingers crossed!

Who to Complain To

- When it comes to purchases made in another EU Member State, whether a camera or a holiday club membership, contact the European Consumer Centre (ECC) Ireland. They can offer advice and if necessary intervene on your behalf with the trader via the network of ECCs across Europe: www. eccireland.ie/01-8797620.
- If you have an unresolved complaint against your telecoms provider contact the Commission for Communications Regulation (Comreg): www.askcomreg.ie/01-8049668/1890-229668.
- If you want further information or guidance on import duties or allowances contact the Revenue Commissioners: www. revenue.ie.

Legislation Name Check

Sale of goods

EC Directive 99/44/EC: Incorporated into Irish law by European Communities (Certain Aspects of the Sale of Consumer Goods and Associated Guarantees) Regulations 2003. Statutory Instrument No 11 of 2003.

Timeshare

EC Directive 2008/122/EC: Incorporated into Irish law by European Union (Protection of Consumers in Respect of Timeshare, Long-term Holiday Product, Resale and Exchange Contracts) Regulations 2011. Statutory Instrument No 73 of 2011.

Mobile roaming

EC Regulation No 717/2007: Incorporated into Irish law by Communications (Mobile Telephone Roaming) (Amendment) Regulations 2010. Statutory Instrument No 156 of 2010.

5

Cancelling Contracts

When you think of the word 'contract', you probably think of something serious, or a pretty big purchase: an employment contract, the contract for a house purchase or a marriage contract.

But we enter into consumer contracts every day. Any time you buy something, whether it is a pair of shoes or an apple, you are accepting the retailer's offer to sell you something at a certain price and the deal is sealed when they accept your offer to purchase.

That a consumer contract is now in place means that the retailer has an obligation to you: to provide what was promised and that the product or service performs in the way in which it was described to you.

While it's usually easy to buy something it is sometimes not as easy to pull out of a deal if you change your mind. When it comes to faulty products or a service not provided as promised, your consumer rights entitle you to a remedy including pulling out of the deal and getting a refund (see Chapter 1 on goods and services).

In the case of some consumer contracts you have a legal right to withdraw for any reason without penalty. For other contracts, like those for television or phone services, you need to check the service-provider's rules on cancellation. Otherwise you may end up stuck with a contract you can't get out of.

Your Legal Rights of Withdrawal

These are the situations in which you have consumer law on your side; you can pull out of a contract because the law says you can:

Distance sales

This covers online shopping for goods and services and other sales that take place over a distance, for example by phone or via catalogue.

You have a seven-day cooling-off period where you can contact the seller (in writing) to let them know you are pulling out. You don't have to have any specific reason for cancelling. This right to cancel without penalty extends to thirty days if the retailer or service-provider does not give you all the information they are required to provide by law. (For further details on online shopping, see Chapter 3.)

'Doorstep' selling

This is a sale that takes place after a visit by a tradesman to your door, or one that takes place in your workplace, for example – in other words the deal is concluded away from the business premises of the supplier.

You are entitled to a withdrawal period of seven days, which starts from the day you receive the goods or information on the contract you have signed up to. However, the sale must be worth more than €50 and unsolicited for this right to kick in.

From the end of 2013 new EU legislation will come into force that extends your right of withdrawal to fourteen days for distance sales. Doorstep sales resulting from solicited visits will also be included when the new legislation comes into force.

Timeshare
New timeshare legislation was signed into Irish law in February 2011; under this you have a fourteen-day cooling-off period once a timeshare contract is signed.

This new legislation also covers holiday clubs – membership clubs that offer holidays at discounted prices and in relation to which there have been many consumer problems in the past.

Consumer credit
A new Consumer Credit Directive was signed into Irish law in June 2010, which increases the length of time you have to withdraw from a contract for a loan. You now have a fourteen-day right of withdrawal starting from the time both parties have signed the contract. When it comes to life insurance the right of withdrawal is thirty days.

Furthermore, you cannot waive or sign away this right and the contract can have been completed either at a distance or face-to-face.

What You Need to Know about Cancelling Services
'Buyer beware' is an old cliché but it makes sense and is probably the most useful thing to bear in mind here. Reading the terms and conditions, especially relating to cancellation, is the smart thing to do.

Mobile phone contracts
Many of these contracts have a twelve-month minimum period, although more and more are offering twenty-four month and even thirty-six month contracts. Be aware that some companies advertise

the lower price offered for the longer contracts up front so you notice this price first and may be more likely to buy into a longer contract.

Giving notice

You will have to give approximately thirty days' notice in writing to cancel your contract after the minimum period is up. Make sure you do this more than a month before your contract is up; otherwise, you'll have to pay the extra month.

Is there any way out mid-contract?

You can quit mid-contract but you'll have to pay the rest of your recurring monthly charges until the minimum contract period is up.

Your best hope is that the mobile service-provider changes a significant term of your contract because they will then have breached their contract with you and you can cancel without penalty. There may be a provision in their terms and conditions that some charges may vary to a specified extent but if a particular service is stopped or some big change is introduced you are entitled to cancel. But pay attention to how you have to cancel even in a situation like this. For example, you may still need to give thirty days' notice from the time you were notified of the change.

Your only other option is to downgrade or change to a tariff that suits you better within the initial contract term, although you may be allowed to do this only after a certain period.

Be warned!
Just because you cancel your direct debit with the bank, this does not mean that you have cancelled your contract with the service-provider and they can still come after you for what you owe. Always cancel in writing to the provider.

Television services

Television services are pretty similar to mobile phone services in that you sign up for a particular time period and you are more or less stuck with the service, at least until the minimum contract period is up.

You will have to give approximately one month's notice to cancel your contract: do it before the start of month eleven if you are in a twelve-month contract so you don't have to pay an extra month.

Is there any way out mid-contract?
If you cancel within the minimum contract period, you will either have to pay the remainder of your monthly subscriptions or an early termination charge, whichever is the lesser.

If the provider changes their terms and conditions, for example they withdraw a channel, you have the right to cancel the contract, even within the initial contract period.

But beware the timeframes: you will still need to withdraw in writing and, depending on the terms and conditions of your contract, your period of notice could be as little as seven or as much as thirty days.

Beware of the potential pitfall of paying one year's subscription in advance. I have heard from consumers who had paid for their twelve-month television service in one payment but when they wanted to cancel after the year was up they forgot to give one month's notice. When they belatedly gave their notice to cancel the provider told them that, rather than losing the next month's payment, they would have to forfeit a whole year's payment as their contract was to pay in advance. In these instances the consumers were refunded the extra eleven months that had been paid up front when they complained.

This practice seems unfair so dispute it if it happens to you.

Gyms

More people may be jogging for free in the great outdoors rather than paying to run on a treadmill but if you are a gym member you had better pay attention so that you don't lose your money if you want to opt out.

You may be in a 'rolling contract', according to which, after your six- or twelve-month initial membership expires, your contract simply continues – as do your direct debits – unless you cancel, giving the required notice. This required notice could be anything from one month to three, so if you forget to give the required notice the gym can keep taking payments for that extra period.

Before you join a gym ask what the cancellation policy is and whether the contract is automatically renewed.

In 2008 the National Consumer Agency (NCA) drew up guidelines for gyms, following an increase in the number of complaints received. As a result some gyms no longer engage in 'rolling contracts'. If you're thinking of joining a gym why not ask if they follow the NCA good practice guidelines. You'll find details of the guidelines on www.consumerconnect.ie.

Unfair Terms in Consumer Contracts

You may think many terms in a contract are unfair, especially if you find yourself in the situation of not being able to cancel a contract or realising a few months down the line that the provider can change an element of the service because it was in the terms and conditions.

There is legislation that governs unfair terms in consumer contracts but neither you nor I can ultimately decide that a term is unfair. This decision can be made only by the High Court and cases can be taken only by the National Consumer Agency (NCA), the Consumers' Association of Ireland (CAI) or the Central Bank.

Many consumer contracts these days are standard forms, not negotiated directly with the consumer and basically provided on a 'take it or leave it' basis.

This is why the legislation is there; to ensure there is no imbalance between your rights and obligations and those of the trader and that no term could be to your detriment.

When is a term 'unfair'?

Firstly, a number of things have to be taken into consideration. What was your bargaining strength? Did you engage in any direct negotiation on specific terms? Was the contract for a special order? Has the business treated you fairly? Was the term expressed in plain and intelligible language? Has the trader acted in good faith and been fair and open?

As always, there are exclusions and these are if the term relates to the main subject matter of the contract or the price.

If a term in a contract is found to be unfair, you cannot be bound by this term but you may still be bound by the contract as a whole, assuming that the contract can exist without the offending term.

Examples of unfair terms

The legislation includes a non-exhaustive list of examples, called the 'grey list'. This doesn't mean that these terms are always going to be unfair and other examples will also arise. These are the sorts of things to look for:

- Terms excluding or restricting the liability of the supplier for death or personal injury
- Unequal obligations: for example, the supplier can cancel the contract but the consumer cannot
- The seller retaining prepayments in the event of their cancelling the contract
- Making a consumer pay a disproportionately high sum in

compensation if they cancel early
- Hidden terms not brought to the consumer's attention
- Automatic renewal of the contract without the consumer's agreement or if the deadline for the consumer to give notice is unreasonably early
- Altering unilaterally the terms of the contract or the characteristics of the product or service without any valid reason
- Binding the consumer to terms that he or she had no real opportunity to become acquainted with before signing up to the contract
- Where the supplier has the exclusive right to interpret the contract
- Where the supplier can cancel a contract without reasonable notice except where there are serious grounds for doing so
- Increasing the price without giving the consumer the right to cancel if the price is too high compared to the original price agreed
- Restricting the consumer's right to take legal action and to use any legal remedy available

Who to Complain To

- If your right to withdraw from a contract during a cooling-off period has been denied contact the NCA for advice: National Consumer Agency (NCA): www.consumerconnect.ie/1890-432432/01-4025555.
- If you feel your contract with a service-provider is unfair, or the supplier is not letting you pull out when you have a valid reason, contact the NCA or the Consumers' Association of Ireland (CAI) for advice: www.the cai.ie/01-4978600.
- For any of the above complaints relating to a retailer or service-provider based in another EU Member State contact the ECC Ireland for advice and their intervention if needed: European Consumer Centre (ECC) Ireland/www.eccireland.ie/01-8797620.

If you have a complaint that you can't resolve yourself the small claims procedure is a remedy: www.courts.ie.

Legislation Name Check

Distance sales

EC Directive 97/7/EC: incorporated into Irish law by the EC (Protection of Consumers in respect of contracts made by means of distance communication) Regulations 2001. Statutory Instrument No 207 of 2001.

Doorstep selling

Directive 85/577/EEC: Incorporated into Irish law by the EC (Cancellation of contracts negotiated away from business premises) Regulations 1989. Statutory Instrument No 224 of 1989.

Timeshare

EC Directive 2008/48/EC: Incorporated into Irish law by EC (Protection of consumers in respect of timeshare, long term holiday products, resale and exchange contracts) Regulations 2011. Statutory Instrument No 73 of 2011.

Consumer credit

EC Directive 2008/48/EC: Incorporated into Irish law by EC (Consumer credit agreements) Regulations 2010. Statutory Instrument No 281 of 2010.

Unfair terms in consumer contracts

EC Directive 93/13/EEC: Incorporated into Irish law by EC (Unfair Terms in Consumer Contracts) Regulations, Statutory Instrument No 27 of 1995, as amended by the European Communities (Unfair Terms in Consumer Contracts) (Amendment) Regulations 2000. Statutory Instrument No 307 of 2000.

6

Switching Service-Providers

We no longer live in a country with one energy supplier and one phone supplier, which means that we all have to get used to looking for the best deals and switching whenever we find a better option. This attitude should also apply to banking and insurance services.

Remember that you have no allegiance to any service-provider. You are their customer and that is all. If you can find a better service, product or price elsewhere, go for it.

In this Chapter
- Phone and internet services
- Television services
- Energy services
- Banking
- Insurance
- Who to complain to
- Legislation name check

Phone and Internet Services

Before you go trawling through websites for the best deals you have to do a bit of homework. You have to know your usage patterns before you can make an informed decision. One package does not fit all – it depends on your circumstances – but you'd be forgiven for thinking that phone/internet providers are deliberately trying to bamboozle us, such is the array of plans available. Yes, it's confusing but follow the guide below to get the best deal for you.

Ask yourself the following questions:
- How many local calls to landlines do I make?
- How many national calls to landlines do I make?
- How many international calls do I make?
- How many calls to mobiles do I make?
- Do I use the landline during the day or just in the evening?
- Do I need a landline at all?
- Do I use broadband?
- What is the broadband availability in my area?
- Do I need 'always on' broadband or do I use the internet only very occasionally?
- What download speed do I need – standard or heavier use?

To bundle or not to bundle?
If you are satisfied that you need a landline and you want broadband at home, then the next question you need to ask yourself is whether to buy these services 'bundled' or separately.

'Bundled' simply means that you are buying a package that provides your landline and broadband needs together. Do you want one bill or two? It depends on your needs and on broadband availability in your area. You may opt for broadband via your phone line, television cable or satellite, for example.

Mobile phones

To find out which phone, mobile or broadband service has the best price to suit your needs, use the comparison tool at www.callcosts.ie.

You are free to switch mobile phone provider and keep the same number. As with fixed line phones, firstly you need to know how you use your phone. You should ask yourself these key questions:

- How many minutes of calls do I make and how many texts do I send? (If you don't have a bill to check, ask your provider to

check your records.)
- Which payment scheme do I want – prepay or billpay?
- Which additional services do I want, for example, internet connection?
- Do I travel abroad and use my phone in other countries?
- Which of the available tariffs fits my usage pattern?

If you don't know the answers to these questions you could well be paying too much for your mobile phone service. For example, if you are on a package that allows you too few minutes for your needs you will be paying through the nose for the additional calls. Conversely, if you are on a deal that gives you too many minutes, you will be paying a higher monthly tariff for nothing.

Before switching you should also consider the following:

- Connection charges
- Monthly tariff
- Call costs (usually per minute or per second rates if you go over your allocation)
- Disconnection and reconnection charges
- Contract termination fees
- Roaming deals available
- Eligibility for upgrades
- Any extras available, like internet access, free or charged

Remember that when you sign up you may be committing to a twelve-month or twenty-four month contract. There will be penalties if you want to leave the contract within that timeframe so take your time to make your mind up. For more information about cancelling contracts, see Chapter 5.

Television Services
There is a myriad options available to you when choosing your television service. Really it all comes down to deciding which channels you want to receive and how many.

If you have a television set you are obliged to pay the licence fee. Everyone in Ireland is entitled to receive free-to-air television, which gives us the Irish channels.

By the end of 2012 analogue television will have been switched off across Europe according to European legislation. In Ireland a switch-over date of 26 October 2012 has been set. At the time of writing the old (analogue) and new (digital) systems are working in tandem, with 92 per cent digital coverage across the country.

Television reception options
Use an aerial
If you just want the Irish channels and don't want to pay, use an aerial. You need to buy a Saorview set-top box to receive the new digital signal.

Free-to-air satellite
This is the fastest-growing market as there are no monthly sub-scriptions and you get plenty of channels. With free-to-air you buy a box and a satellite dish for a one-off fee. This system doesn't come with Irish channels so you'll need an aerial for these. Alternatively, you can buy a combination freesat and Saorview-compatible set-top box for use with or without a dish or aerial. Although analogue television will not be switched off until 26 October 2012, if you are buying anything now make sure it's Saorview compatible.

Get a paid subscription service
You can pay for a subscription service with Sky or UPC, for example, and get a basic package, including the Irish and British channels, with the option of add-ons such as movie and sports channels. If you subscribe to this type of service you will not need to do anything to receive digital TV.

Watch television online
If you want to forego having a television set you can still watch television on your computer. There are websites (like aertv.ie) that

provide free access to Irish channels and access to other channels on a paid basis.

Location, location

Admittedly, you are unlikely to move house just to receive more free television channels but if you live near the border with Northern Ireland or in the south-east of the country you will most likely receive the UK channels free.

> Remember: if you are buying a new television now make sure it is an integrated digital television (iDtelevision), as this will allow you to receive the free digital service without a set-top box. Also make sure it is Mpeg 4 compatible, as this is the system Ireland is using for digital television services. It is also recommended to buy one that is Saorview approved. Check out www.saorview.ie for further details.

Energy Services

Thanks to EU legislation, Europe's energy market has been de-regulated since 2007, meaning that we have a choice about who supplies our gas and electricity. It took a while for more service suppliers to come on board and it wasn't until 2011 that the electricity market in Ireland became fully deregulated when the ESB (now ESB Electric Ireland), became free to compete on price.

The European Commission is now working on developing a single market for energy in Europe with new legislation passed in 2011.

Currently, in Ireland, private customers can choose between ESB Electric Ireland, Bord Gáis, Airtricity and Flogas as energy suppliers The rates charged change all the time and it's quite complicated to compare the different tariffs and packages.

Just as with your phone, you need to know your usage requirements – whether you use more gas than electricity and your daily patterns of usage. Some providers offer competitive packages if you buy both electricity and gas from them but usually the deal is better for one energy source than the other. There is no point in signing up for a combined deal of cheap gas and not-so-cheap electricity if you use more electricity than gas.

Likewise there are usually different urban and rural tariffs and day- and night-time rates so you need to choose the plan that is right for you.

What you need to know about switching energy provider

- No work is required to change electricity supplier; it's the same wires and same plugs.
- Check to see if there is a minimum contract, in which case you'll have to stay with that provider until the contract period runs out unless you want to pay a penalty for leaving early.
- To switch you will need to call or go online and quote your MPRN number or GPRN numbers, which you will find at the top of your bill. These are the numbers that identify your connection and are unique to your home.
- To speed up the process you should take a meter reading yourself at the time of switching and pass that information on to your new supplier.
- Pensioners and other customers who have state-sponsored discounts can avail of an identical service from all providers.
- ESB Networks is an independent company and still owns and operates the electricity infrastructure in Ireland. It continues to read meters and provide an emergency call-out service, no matter which provider you are with.

Comparing the deals on offer is not always easy. You have to wade through: day and night rates; urban and rural rates; different rates depending how you pay or get your bill; different standing charges and stand-alone or combined electricity and gas deals.

For example, some deals with cheaper tariffs may have a higher standing charge so this may not suit you if you are a low electricity user (i.e. below the average 5300 KwH per year for electricity). For combined gas and electricity deals, one is usually cheaper that the other but there is no point in signing up for cheaper electricity and not so cheap gas if you use more gas. Usually the best 'discounts' are for customers who are happy to receive e-bills and pay by direct debit. But remember when it comes to 'discounts' for electricity the percentage discounts are taken off different standard rates, so are not always directly comparable from provider to provider. When it comes to gas services, gas prices charged by Bord Gáis are still regulated by the Commission for Energy Regulation, so other providers calculate their percentage 'discounts' on that regulated tariff.

At the time of writing the Commission for Energy Regulation is devising an accreditation system for websites that provide energy price comparisons. Once this system comes into place, use only accredited sites. The best bet at the moment is www.bonkers.ie.

Debt hoppers

If you are a debt hopper – someone who switches energy suppliers, leaving unpaid bills behind – be warned that new legislation to tackle this came into force on 1 October 2011. Energy companies are allowed to warn a new supplier if a domestic customer owes more than €250 and is sixty days overdue. They are not allowed to block someone from switching and the customer will only be 'flagged' to the other provider. The other company won't be given any further information, such as whether you owe €5 or €1000 or have negotiated a payment plan, but it's still information they may use in their assessment of you as a customer.

Banking

The banks subscribe to a voluntary code of practice that enables you to switch your personal account from one bank to another. This covers current accounts and deposit or savings accounts where you don't have to give advance notice to withdraw funds.

What you should do

- Bring along a proof of identity (passport or driver's licence) and proof of address such as a bill.
- Ask your new bank for its 'switching pack', which will take you through the process.
- You should fill out an account transfer form. This will allow the new bank to transfer your balance and set up any existing standing orders or direct debits on your new account.
- The new bank should also give you: a copy of the terms and conditions; details of fees, charges and interest rates; and a point of contact for queries.
- Once your application is approved your new account should be up and running in ten working days.

Insurance

If you drive a car you are legally obliged to have motor insurance and if you have a mortgage your mortgage provider will contract-ually oblige you to have buildings insurance and life insurance. Other than that, whether you buy an insurance policy is up to you. If you do decide to buy one, it is essential that it should suit your needs.

Price may be the driving factor but it shouldn't be the only one. It's what is inside the policy that really counts and even more so the exclusions – in other words the things the policy won't cover at all.

With the cost of premiums going up and down all the time, you should review all your policies annually to see if you can save money and get better cover. Always ask for a better deal than the quote you are given. You'll be surprised how much that quote can be reduced.

The following is a guide to the sort of things you should take into consideration when you are seeking a quote or checking a policy in the main insurance categories.

Home insurance

Rebuilding costs

Reducing rebuilding costs can lower premiums so make sure that yours are not too high. This is especially important given the decreases in rebuilding costs in recent years. Remember too that if your rebuild costs are too high your premium will be higher but this does not mean that you'll get any more money if you have to make a claim. Nor is it a good idea to underestimate rebuilding costs: if you're underinsured you will not be compensated for the full value of what you have lost.

Contents

When it comes to insuring your contents make sure that you aren't over-insured. You are insuring 'moveable' items, including furniture, carpets and curtains, as well as all your clothes and electronics: in other words things that will come under replacement costs and not fixtures or fittings. If you are buying insurance online, be alert to drop-down boxes that suggest you add on extras for expensive items or for items left permanently in the garden. By all means itemise the value of expensive things like your engagement ring but make sure the amount you have chosen for your general contents has not already taken these values into account, or you'll end up over-insured and paying too much.

All-risks cover

All-risks cover insures your belongings outside the home and is an optional extra under most home insurance policies. It protects against loss or theft of, or accidental damage to, personal valuables such as jewellery. Not everything will automatically be covered, including items commonly taken outside the home such as laptops, hearing aids and mobile phones, which you may have to list as specified items.

Excess

One of the first things you should check when considering switching is the amount for excess charged. This is the amount of any claim made that you will have to pay yourself. Excesses typically range from €125 up to €500: this could well amount to more than the value of an item you are claiming for. It's also worth considering the impact that making a claim for a relatively low-value item will have on your no-claims bonus and future premiums, which tend to rise as a result of claims.

Security

If you have a monitored alarm or have recently upgraded yours tell your insurance provider as this will reduce your premium. Some firms provide a burglar-alarm discount but be careful: if the house was unoccupied at the time of a burglary and the alarm wasn't on you may not be covered, according to the terms of the policy.

Claims history

Some companies will not give you a quote if you have made a claim or number of claims within a specified number of years or to a specified amount. This will limit your choice, but under no circumstances should you not tell a new provider that you made a claim in the past. They will find out eventually and if you haven't disclosed something it could mean they won't cover you for a claim or it may make your contract with them null and void.

Flooding

Many insurance companies will not provide flood cover for customers who have recently claimed for flood damage. If you are having problems obtaining a quote the only thing you can do is to approach a specialist broker who can offer you advice and assistance.

Leaving your home

Most policies include a clause that stipulates that your home won't be covered if you are away for more than twenty-eight or thirty days. (You can get more expensive policies that cover up to forty-five days). If you plan to go away make sure you contact your provider and ask their advice on what to do. This could mean ensuring that someone checks your home regularly or buying extra cover.

For regular cost comparison surveys on home and motor insurance go to www.itsyourmoney.ie.

Motor Insurance
Type of cover
The cost of the premium will depend on your age and other factors and also on type of cover you want. Third-party cover pays out for claims that other people make against you for damage or injury caused by your driving; third-party, fire and theft cover also allows you to claim for loss or damage to your own car as a result of fire or theft; comprehensive cover gives you third-party, fire and theft cover and also covers damage to your car, no matter who is to blame. You'll also want to check out what else is covered: windscreen and glass cover; damaged or stolen personal belongings; recovery service and emergency breakdown assistance; third-party cover when driving other cars; replacement or hired car if your own car is off the road.

The value of your car
As the value of your car is depreciating all the time, make sure to change its value on your insurance policy when you renew each year. Otherwise your premium may be higher than it needs to be.

Holding a full licence
Whether you have a full or provisional licence will also affect the cost of insurance, as will your age and gender, how many years you have been driving and if you have driving convictions or penalty points.

Where you keep your car
It's always worth mentioning to insurers if your car is kept in a locked garage or underground car park, or if the area you live in has Neighbourhood Watch or a Garda station nearby. Any of these could affect the price of the policy.

What you mightn't be covered for
The most common scenario is that you were negligent about something, like leaving the keys in the ignition of the car while you pop back into the house; damaging your car when driving off-road if your policy doesn't cover it; or stolen belongings unless they were securely out of view, for example in a locked boot.

Travel insurance
Travel insurance may cover you for some costs if you suffer loss, damage or delay of luggage, cancelled flights, delayed or missed departure, curtailments of your trip, loss or theft of money or passport and illness or injury. It will also cover you for medical expenses and personal injury or accident, hospital cover and repatriation. As always you should check the exclusions.

Cancellation
If you need to cancel a trip or come home early due to your own illness or that of a family member, your policy will not cover you for an existing illness unless you disclosed it before purchasing the policy and they accepted this. This is by far the biggest complaint area. It may cost you more but you will have to tell the insurer in advance and get extra cover in order to avoid disappointment later.

Remember also to check the level of cover for cancellation; there is no point in having cancellation cover of €1500 if your holiday cost €5000. And remember: if you buy annual multi-trip cover that starts on the date of your holiday, you will not be covered for cancellation until the policy has started.

Redundancy
If you are worried about losing your job check your travel insurance. Some policies will cover you against redundancy but only if you did not know your job was under threat when you bought the policy.

Missed connections
Some policies will cover for missed connections of flights or

cruises so if you are concerned about this possibility, make sure it's included in your policy. Bear in mind that missed connection cover often applies only if you have left a certain length of time between connections, for example, three hours.

Sports
A standard policy will cover you for basic activities but you will need extra cover for winter sports or extreme sports and also for golf equipment. Nor will general travel insurance normally cover you for sporting competitions. If you intend to take part in sporting activities, check the terms of the policy before you buy.

Theft
Your policy will require you to prove any theft so remember that you have to report losses or theft quickly to the local police, hotel or tour representative. Check if you have to inform the insurer immediately. If so, keep the relevant contact numbers with you. Be aware that some insurers will not cover you for loss or theft of belongings if you have been negligent – so do be careful with your things.

If you're buying a package holiday the travel agent or tour operator can insist that you have travel cover but you don't have to buy their insurance, so shop around for the best deal.

Luggage
If your luggage is lost you can claim from the airline but if that doesn't get you anywhere you can claim from your travel insurance. Insurers will generally look for receipts and/or credit card statements to confirm the value of lost contents. Some policies may cap the amount of loss claimed for each separate item at anything from €90 to €250 and they may exclude items such as ipods and cameras.

Injury and illness
Amounts that will be paid to cover personal injury and medical claims vary widely from policy to policy, from €1 million to €5

million. Personal injury cover could be €20,000 or €70,000. Check if you have cover for illness or injury abroad under your private health insurance policy to make sure you are not buying the same thing twice but first check whether the cover under your own health insurance policy is sufficient. Your travel insurance policy will be cheaper if you exclude injury and illness cover abroad because you are already covered by your private health insurance policy. But be sure to check the policy first.

Airline failure
Some brokers advise that customers should look for cover for airline failure and third party suppliers (hotel, car hire) in case any of those businesses collapses.

Excess
All policies charge an excess before you can make most claims. This could be as little as €25 or as much as €100. Find out what the excess is. Some policies allow you to buy an 'excess waiver', for around €8-€10; this means that you won't have to pay the excess charge if you are making a claim.

Health insurance
Private health insurance has become an expensive option for many, with thousands exiting their plans because of increased premiums. If you want to keep some level of cover you can switch suppliers to get a better deal. We all have the right to switch and if you are in the middle of treatment, this cannot be interrupted. Health insurance providers cannot refuse us cover and premiums cannot be weighted against your age or a pre-existing health condition.

- If you switch health insurers and retain the same level of cover nothing will change except the premium you pay.
- If you switch and upgrade your cover a waiting period may apply before any new additional benefits kick in (a maximum of two years if you are under sixty-five; a maximum of five years if you are over sixty-five, fifty-two weeks for maternity

cover).

- If you switch and downgrade your cover, a waiting period may apply if you upgrade again in the future.
- If you quit and leave a gap of thirteen weeks or more before signing up for a policy again you will be treated as a brand new customer and waiting periods will apply. These are: twenty-six weeks if you are under fifty-five, fifty-five weeks if you are aged between fifty-five and sixty-five and two years if you are aged sixty-five or over. However, you will be covered in the event of an accident or injury that occurs while you wait for full cover.
- The waiting periods for new customers are much longer if you have a pre-existing illness (five years under fifty-five; seven years for fifty-five-fifty-nine; ten years if you are over sixty).

For comprehensive policy and price comparisons of health insurance and health cashplan products take a look at www.hia.ie.

Saving money on private health cover
- One way is to downgrade cover but make sure the cover is adequate and take into account the waiting periods that will kick in if you want to upgrade again. Consider whether your children benefit from private cover.
- If the provider you are with announces that they are increasing premiums from a certain date, renew your policy before that happens in order to take advantage of the lower premium rate for a further twelve months. The closer to your renewal date you are the more sense this makes.
- Switch to a company or corporate plan, as these tend to be cheaper than other plans but with the same level of cover. All policy-providers sell company plans but they are marketed to businesses, not generally advertised. However, by law they must be available to all.
- Switch to a health cash plan or mix and match between private cover and a cash plan. Cash plans cover day-to-day outpatient expenses rather than in-patient or procedure expenses. You

can claim for a cash benefit that may be a flat rate or related to the cost of the service provided, after a consultation or treatment has taken place and the bill has been settled.

In June 2011 the VHI began to impose penalties if you cancel your contract with them within your contract period. If no claims have been paid you will have to pay the health insurance levy (calculated on a pro-rata basis) and an administration fee of €50. If a claim has been paid you will have to pay the outstanding premium due until the renewal date.

Who to Complain To

For complaints relating to communications services:
Commission for Communication Regulation (Comreg); www.askcomreg.ie/1890-229 668/01-8049668

For complaints relating to the provision of energy supply:
Commission for Energy Regulation; www.energycustomers.ie/1890-404404

For unresolved complaints relating to insurance:
The Financial Services Ombudsman; www.financialombudsman.ie/1890-882-090/01- 6620899

For further information on the switchover to digital television:
www.saorview.ie/locall: 1890-222012

Legislation Name Check

Broadcasting Act 2009, Statutory Instrument No 18 of 2005.

7

Buying and Servicing a Car

After a house, a car is likely to be your next biggest purchase and this is why the subject of buying and servicing a car deserves a special chapter. It may be hard to believe that your rights when buying a car come under the same legislation as if you were buying a frock or a fridge.

But given the amount of money often involved and, for the consumer, the importance of safety when it comes to motor vehicles, resolving complaints isn't always as easy as it should be.

In this Chapter
- Your rights when buying a car
- What to look out for as a buyer
- Cars bought abroad
- Car checks
- Car repairs and servicing
- Who to complain to
- Legislation name check

Your Rights when Buying a Car

Just as with any other product, when you buy a car, either new or second hand, the car must be:

- Of merchantable quality
- Fit for its purpose
- As described

- Roadworthy

In addition it is an offence to provide false or misleading information about the car, such as the car's history, specification and the need for any repair work. It is also an offence to omit or conceal any information regarding the main characteristics of a car.

Dealers also have to provide truthful information about their own services, for example any after-sales service they may provide or if they have membership of a trade organisation.

Remember that if you buy from a private seller you are not covered by consumer law but a seller is still required to give you honest information about the car. If something goes wrong when you buy from a private individual, your only option in the case of an unresolved dispute is to pursue a civil action in the courts.

If you are driving a car it must be in roadworthy condition. It is illegal to drive a car:

- With tyres that are beloow the minimum standard tread depth of 1.6mm
- With defective lighting
- Wihout compliant licence plates
- That is untaxed, uninsured or not registered
- That doesn't display a valid NCT disk, once the car is more than four years old

---

What to Look Out For as a Buyer

When it comes to second-hand cars you would do well to carry out plenty of research and check all the facts before buying. It's also a good idea to ask the dealer a lot of questions and get the answers in writing so that you will have evidence at your disposal if you need it later.

Top Tips

- View the car in daylight, preferably in dry conditions, so that you see any scrapes or scratches clearly.
- Check for rust, tyres not of the same make and any sign of leaks.
- Check functions such as lights, doors and wipers.
- Bring a mechanic to look over the car and take it for a road test.

Cars Bought Abroad

According to the European Consumer Centre most complaints about cars purchased abroad relate to problems getting repairs done. If you are buying a car abroad you should ask whether services can be carried out locally at the seller's expense rather than your having to bring the car back to where you bought it. Get any agreement in writing.

Also ask about the scope of any warranties offered, as a UK warranty may not apply in Ireland and this will make it difficult to get assistance.

Some Irish people buy a car from the UK over the phone, without seeing it and on nothing more than the verbal assurances of the seller. You should always get details in writing before making a commitment to buy.

VAT and Vehicle Registration Tax on cars bought abroad

If you buy your car in another EU Member State you do not pay VAT in that country. You pay VAT in Ireland and it is calculated on the Irish list price of the car and not the amount you actually paid.

In Ireland you also have to pay Vehicle Registration Tax (VRT). VRT payable is a percentage of the expected retail price including all taxes in the state. This price is called the 'Open Market Selling Price' (OMSP).

If you buy a used car in another Member State make sure to get the vehicle registration document or a certificate of permanent export, which you should bring with you to the Revenue Vehicle Registration Office. Bring your car to this office not later than the working day following your arrival in Ireland. You should complete a Declaration for Registration form and pay the Vehicle Registration Tax (VRT) charged after inspection. You will receive a receipt for the VRT paid, showing the registration number assigned to your car. A vehicle registration certificate will be posted within two to three days and you must display the correct registration plates on your car within three days of the date of registration. Contact your local VRT office for further details: www.revenue.ie.

Car Checks

There are many things to look out for. If you are buying from a garage that is a member of the Society of the Irish Motor Industry (SIMI) ask for a car history check, as this service is available from all SIMI members. This check will include information on: outstanding finance; import information; UK data on stolen, scrapped or written-off cars; the number of previous owners; if the vehicle was ever a hackney or taxi; and NCT data.

You can pay for a service that searches for the car's history on your behalf and you can also buy a car inspection or engineer's report from many companies. You can do this online at sites such as motorcheck.ie, carsireland.ie, cartell.ie, aaireland.ie, mywheels.ie and carhistorycheck.ie. On these sites you may be able to carry out a check for UK registered cars. Consult hpicheck.com for UK cars specifically.

Checklist
Registration Certificate
Always check all vehicle paperwork thoroughly before proceeding with a purchase. Cross-reference the model, colour and year of registration with the certificate. Are the name and address of the current vendor the same as the details on the certificate? Ensure

that the appropriate sections of the certificate are completed before finalising the purchase of the vehicle.

Chassis Number
Check that the chassis number (usually seventeen digits) on the vehicle matches the chassis number on the registration certificate. The chassis number is a unique number given to a vehicle by the manufacturer. It can be found in several locations throughout the vehicle, usually on the windscreen, in the engine bay or on the driver's door near the lock. If the chassis number is absent or damaged, exercise extreme caution as this could mean that the vehicle was stolen.

Keys
How many keys are available for the vehicle? There are usually two or three. Do all the keys open all doors?

Owners
How many owners have there been? If there have been several over a short period of timeframe, it may indicate an unreliable vehicle.

You should be satisfied that the car hasn't been 'clocked'. Clocking is the practice of changing the genuine odometer reading of the car, which tells you how many miles or kilometres the car has travelled. The odometer will be manipulated to give a lower reading, making the car more attractive to a buyer.

The average annual mileage on privately-owned petrol cars in Ireland is estimated at 16,000 km (10,000 miles), or about 24,000km (15,000 miles) for diesel cars. So if the car is some years old and shows sign of heavy wear and tear but the mileage is low, be on your guard.

This practice is illegal. If you discover it, report it to the National Consumer Agency.

Mileage
Use the odometer readings on past NCT certificates and the service history to verify that the current odometer reading is roughly what you would expect it to be.

Service Details
If there are lots of service receipts this may be indicative of persistent problems with the car. If there are no receipts at all, proceed with caution as it may be difficult to resell the car without receipts to prove the service history.

Bodywork
There may or may not be evidence of bodywork on the car. Always ask the vendor if the car was ever crashed. If the car has had an accident ask for details of the accident and the car's repair to be put on the invoice if you decide to proceed with the purchase. Some cars that had been crashed in the UK have found their way on to the Irish market so be careful.

Outstanding Finance
Outstanding finance is one of the biggest risks facing used-car buyers. If it remains unpaid when you buy the car, you may not actually own it and it may be seized by the finance company. You can check out the situation on hpifirst.ie (for a fee) or the car-check websites mentioned above should include this information when you pay for a car-history check.

Remember that if you buy from a private seller you are not covered by consumer law but a seller is still required to give you honest information about the car. If something goes wrong when you buy from a private seller, your only option in the case of an unresolved dispute is to pursue a civil action in the courts.

Car Repairs and Servicing
Thanks to EU legislation the European car market for sales and servicing is an open one. The legislation allows independent garages

access to the manufacturers' data needed to carry out repairs so that you have the choice to shop around for the best value. Ask independent garages which make of car they focus on. They have to pay for the information that allows them to diagnose problems with your car so they often focus on specific brands.

Since June 2010, when updated 'block exemption' rules for competition in the car sector were introduced, manufacturers cannot make your warranty conditional on having the car serviced in an authorised garage only. This means you can shop around for the best service deal. However, manufacturers can request that repairs carried our under warranty and paid for by them are carried out within their authorised network.

You are also free to buy spare parts from an independent seller, without this affecting your warranty, although the parts should be of appropriate standard. When it comes to car parts bear in mind that manufacturers do not always make all the parts themselves so you could buy exactly the same part or an equivalent one from an independent seller for less than an authorised seller would charge.

What to look out for
Black economy/backstreet repairs
You should choose a garage or mechanic who has a good reputation or on the basis of a direct recommendation from someone you trust. Beware of any business or individual that deals in cash only and won't issue receipts.

You should be very cautious about getting a car repaired by a trader who has no premises or trading address and should always ask if the work will be covered by a written guarantee. If it isn't, consider taking your business elsewhere.

Price/additional work
Some dealers advertise services at a set price. Before signing up for deals like this, you should check what is included and what is not.

Spending a little time doing research can often be the quickest route to the best value. Make sure before you agree to the service that you ask how much it will cost and what it will cover. Prices can vary hugely between independent and branded garages so ask questions before you make your decision.

It is illegal for a trader to claim that work needs to be carried out when it doesn't. Make sure you are clear in instructing your mechanic not to do any additional work on the car without consulting you and don't be afraid to get a second opinion if you think some work may be unnecessary or if the price quoted strikes you as high.

Pre-NCT test

There is a school of thought that suggests it is a good idea to have your car serviced before its NCT. However, before deciding to do a pre-NCT, you should weigh up the likelihood of your car failing and the net benefit of spending money on a service with no guarantee of passing. Some people operate on the basis that the NCT will identify any particular problem areas that can then be remedied by their mechanic. If you routinely have your car serviced, it should be in appropriate roadworthy condition. Do the sums and see which option makes more sense in your circumstances.

Who to Complain To

The garage

Whether it's a defective car, a case of misinformation or a car service that didn't do the job, your first port of call should always be the garage where you bought the car or got the repair work carried out. Your statutory rights oblige the garage to provide a remedy, although they will generally refer you to your manufacturer's guarantee if you have one. If you don't have one or if it has expired, you still have your statutory rights so insist on the garage providing a remedy.

For advice and to resolve disputes

- For advice on your rights and also to report an instance of, for example, car clocking, contact the National Consumer Agency (NCA): www.consumerconnect.ie/1890-432432/01-4025555. For information of your consumer rights you can contact the Consumers' Association of Ireland: www.thecai.ie; 01-4978600.
- For problems with cars or car parts bought within the EU, contact the European Consumer Centre (ECC): www.eccireland.ie/01-8797620.
- If the garage where you bought the car or paid for a service or repair is a member of Society of the Irish Motor Industry (SIMI), you can use their disputes procedure – www.simi.ie/01-6761690 – or call the Chartered Institute of Arbitrations (they arrange the scheme) directly at 01-7079739.
- If your claim is for less than €2000, you can submit an application against the garage in question to the small claims court: www.courts.ie. See Chapter 18.

Legislation Name Check

Sale of goods and services

Sale of Goods and Supply of Services Act 1980

EC Directive 99/44/EC: Incorporated into Irish law by European Communities (Certain Aspects of the Sale of Consumer Goods and Associated Guarantees) Regulations 2003. Statutory Instrument No 11 of 2003).

Misleading information

Directive 2005/29/EC on unfair business-to-consumer commercial practices in the internal market was transposed into Irish law by the Consumer Protection Act 2007 (No 19 of 2007).

Car selling and servicing

Commission Regulation (EC) No 1400/2002 of 31 July 2002 on the application of Article 81(3) of the Treaty to categories of vertical agreements and concerted practices in the motor vehicle sector. (Expires 31st May 2013).

Commission Regulation (EU) No 461/2010 of 27 May 2010 on the application of Article 101(3) of the Treaty on the Functioning of the European Union to categories of vertical agreements and concerted practices in the motor vehicle sector.

8

Paying for a Car with Credit

When you buy a car, the chances are you will need to get your hands on some money to pay for it. You could get a bank or credit union loan, use a loan offered by the garage called a 'credit sale agreement' or enter into a hire purchase or leasing agreement with the garage.

When you get a bank or credit union loan, it is obvious that your agreement is with them. But when you opt for a payment agreement with the garage your contract will also be with the financial institution; the garage is just acting as an intermediary and will earn a commission or payment for this. Before you choose your method of payment you need to know what the differences are and what liabilities you have if you can't afford the car any longer.

In this Chapter
- Payment options
- Hire purchase explained
- Pulling out early
- Repossession
- Tips
- Credit checks
- Who to complain to
- Legislation name check

Payment Options
Bank/credit union loan
As you are borrowing money to pay for the car in full, you will own

it from day one. If you have problems with repayments you should discuss restructuring the loan with your lender. As you own the car you have the option of selling it to pay off the balance of your loan, or part of it, unlike a hire purchase agreement, for example.

Credit sale agreement
You own the car once you sign the deal but check the terms and conditions carefully as these agreements can involve hefty fees.

Hire purchase
You own the car only when you have made the final payment. Up until that point you are merely hiring it. There are hefty fees and inflexibility if you have trouble meeting payments.

Lease agreement
You will never own the car: you are just renting it for an agreed period of time. Some consumer hire agreements allow you to purchase at the end of the agreed term.

> You can't use the APR (annual percentage rate) to compare the cost of a hire purchase agreement with the cost of a loan, as hire purchase agreements do not have to show APRs. Instead, add up the total amount you have to pay, plus interest and any additional fees and charges, to find out the true cost.

Hire Purchase Explained
This is worth explaining in some detail as hire purchase agreements are complicated, with the result that you can get yourself into a lot of trouble if you don't understand what you are signing up to.

Hire purchase is a finance agreement where you pay a monthly amount over a fixed period to 'hire' the product, let's say a car. You 'purchase' the car when you make your final repayment, so until that time the car finance company actually owns the car, not you. This means that if you run into financial difficulties you cannot sell the car to repay the debt.

In addition to interest on repayments, there are other fees associated with hire purchase. For example, there is a setting-up fee of between €50 and €70; interest surcharge on missed payments; a completion fee of around €60; a rescheduling fee of around €60 and a repossession fee of around €300.

Information you must receive

Within ten days of making an agreement with a hire purchase company you must receive a copy of the agreement in writing. It should clearly be marked 'hire purchase' so that you are in no doubt as to what type of agreement you have signed up to.

The information must include:

- A description of the car
- The price of the car and the amount, number and schedule of instalments, you have to pay
- The total hire purchase price; including all instalments, interest, deposits and fees
- That you have a cooling-off period of ten days when you are entitled to pull out of the agreement
- Restrictions and penalties for not sticking to the agreed terms
- Information on repossession
- Information on the 'half rule' and 'one-third rule' relating to pulling out of the contract (terms explained below)

If you buy a car by means a hire purchase agreement, although you don't own it, if it turns out to be faulty, the garage is still liable to provide a remedy: for example, repair, replacement or refund.

Pulling Out Early

You can pull out of the hire purchase contract early but it all depends on how much of the original hire purchase price you have paid.

- If you have paid half or more of the hire purchase price, you are entitled to end the agreement under the 'half rule' and

return the car.
- If you are in arrears but have paid more than half you can still end the agreement but you will have to pay the arrears owed.

To end your agreement under the half rule you must write to your provider informing them of this.

- Agree a pick-up or return point to avoid a collection fee.
- Take pictures of the car inside and out to confirm its condition.
- If repairs are needed get them done yourself as the provider may charge you more if they do it.
- Do not sign a voluntary surrender form as you would be giving up your right to return the car under the half rule.

If you haven't paid half but cannot afford to keep up re-payments on the car, that you can 'voluntarily surrender' the car, by signing a voluntary surrender form. In this case the finance company will sell the car and the money made will go towards your debt but you will still have to make repayments until the remaining debt is paid off.

Balloon payments

Look out for what are known as 'balloon payments'. This is a system in which monthly repayments are not evenly spread out and you have a large final payment at the end of the term. This will mean that your initial monthly repayments are smaller and more affordable but it will take you longer to get to the halfway stage, where you have the option of pulling out if you can no longer afford to pay.

Repossession

If you have paid less than one-third of the total and have missed repayments the car finance company can repossess the car without taking legal action. You'll still be liable for what's owed plus the repossession fee and any other fees that may apply, such as towing and trace fees.

If you have paid one-third of the hire purchase price, a lender cannot repossess the car without taking legal action against you.

Tips

- Before you sign a hire purchase agreement, read the terms and conditions carefully so you are clear about what you are signing up for. Make sure it is a consumer agreement and not a commercial hire-purchase agreement.
- If you are having difficulty making your monthly repayments check if you have signed up for payment protection insurance with your original hire-purchase agreement, as you may be eligible to have your repayments made for a time, depending on your circumstances.
- If at all possible try to bring repayment to half the hire-purchase price as then you can walk away under the 'half rule'.
- If you can't bring payments up to half and cannot reschedule and must give up the car, surrender it voluntarily rather that wait for repossession as it will be cheaper. Either way you'll still be liable for what you owe.

Credit Checks

No matter which sort of credit agreement you are entering into the financial institution may carry out a credit history check on you to see how likely you are to meet repayments or to default. Most people find out that there is a problem with their credit history only after they apply for a loan and by then it may be too late to do anything about it.

How does the credit rating system work?

Most lenders send information on their customers to the Irish Credit Bureau (ICB), although the majority of credit unions do not. When you sign a loan agreement, there is generally a clause in the terms and conditions that says you are giving the bank permission to share your data with the ICB and to access it.

No one can access or share your data without that permission.

You can get a copy of your record from the ICB to make sure that all the information held on you is correct and manage your plan of action if you are thinking of applying for a loan.

Information contained in the credit report

- Your personal contact details and date of birth
- The names of lenders and loan account numbers that are currently active or that were active in the last five years
- Repayments you have made or missed
- Failure to clear loans
- Loans that were settled for less than you owed
- Legal actions your lender took against you and your credit score
- Who has accessed your credit report

The credit report details your loan accounts and clearly sets out your repayment history for each of them over a twenty-four month period. For each month you'll get a 'tick' to indicate that payments are up to date, or a '1' to indicate one month in arrears or '2' for two months in arrears and so on. You will also be given a credit score and the report will explain what the best and lowest scores are so you can see where your score lands.

Armed with this information, if you are having problems getting a credit agreement or loan, you can explain in advance to the bank what happened in a particular situation and try and show that you are responsible and have sorted out repayment schedules. It's all about making yourself look like a better prospect.

The facts on accessing your credit history

- It costs €6 to access your credit report from the Irish Credit Bureau (ICB) and you can apply online (www.icbu.ie) or by phone.
- Your application will take three or four days to process; allow an extra day or two if you want it posted to you rather than emailed.

- You cannot get your credit history over the phone.
- By law financial institutions must ensure that information they hold or give to anyone else about you is correct and up to date so you have the right to insist that they correct any incorrect information about you.
- If you find a mistake in your report, contact the lender and ask them to write to the ICB with details of the change and request a copy of their letter.
- For information on your financial rights and to complain contact the National Consumer Agency: www.itsyourmoney.ie/1890-432432/01-4025555.

If you have acted as a guarantor for a child or a friend and he or she has missed out on payments, your credit record will also be adversely affected. If you are a guarantor make sure you are copied on any correspondence in relation to a loan you have guaranteed so that you will know if repayments are late and can take action if needed.

Who to Complain To

If you have a complaint about an agreement that you haven't been able to resolve with the lender, you can take your complaint to the Financial Services Ombudsman: www.financialombudsman. ie/1890-88 20-90/01-6620899.

If you are in financial difficulties you can get free advice about what to do next if you make an appointment with the Money Advice and Budgeting Service (MABS): www.mabs.ie/1890 83438/01-8129350.

If you have found a mistake on your credit history check and your lender fails to put it right for you, you can make a formal complaint to the Office of the Data Protection Commissioner: www. dataprotection.ie/1890252231/057-8684800.

Legislation Name Check

Hire purchase

Hire Purchase (Amendment) Act 1960. Statutory Instrument No 15 of 1960.

Data protection

There are many pieces of legislation relating to data protection but the main one is: Directive 95/46/EC on the protection of individuals with regard to the processing of personal data and on the free movement of such data. Transposed in Ireland under the Data Protection (Amendment) Act 2003. SI No 6 of 2003.

9

Product Safety

All products sold on the EU market must be safe. They may have been manufactured within or outside the EU but as long as they are on sale in the EU they have to comply with EU product safety standards.

A safe product is defined as a product, including free giveaways and products supplied as part of a service, which 'under normal or reasonably foreseeable conditions of use does not present an undue risk to the health and safety of consumers'.

Some products come with inherent and obvious risks – candles for example – so producers have a duty to provide adequate warnings to the consumer about these dangers and advise on safe use.

In this Chapter
- Product safety rules
- The CE mark
- RAPEX – recalls and enforcement
- Toy safety
- Who to complain to
- Legislation name check

Product Safety Rules
Almost every product put on the market for consumers has to conform to general safety requirements: second-hand products that have antique value or those that need to be repaired are excluded.

A safe product is defined as one that poses no threat, or a reduced threat, in accordance with the nature of its use, and that maintains a high level of protection for the health and safety of consumers.

A product is considered safe once it conforms to the safety provisions provided in EU law, or if there are no specific rules, if the product complies with the national regulations of the country where the product is being marketed or sold and with any voluntary standards in place.

It is important to note the role of businesses: distributors and/ or manufacturers are responsible for ensuring the safety of their products. In order to get a certificate of conformity each product must be tested by an accredited test house. If required, a national authority (such as the National Consumer Agency/NCA in Ireland) can inspect the technical file of any product and carry out their own test.

The obligations of manufacturers and distributors
- To provide consumers with the necessary information with regard to a product's inherent risk
- To take measures to avoid safety risks (for example, engage in safety alerts and recalls)
- To supply products that meet the general safety requirements
- To monitor the safety of products on the market
- To provide the necessary documents to ensure that the products can be traced

Quite apart from the fact that it is clearly in the interest of businesses to put safe products on the market, they are obliged to inform the NCA if a product they have placed on the market is dangerous and this is why the vast majority of safety recalls are voluntary.

Other legislation
In addition to general product safety rules there are many pieces of legislation governing the safety of products. To name a few, there are

specific rules governing low-voltage electrical equipment, personal protection equipment, (like bicycle helmets and life jackets) and gas-burning appliances.

In July 2011 new toy-safety legislation entered into force, providing for enhanced protection in relation to toys. This is particularly significant given that the number-one category of product recalls in the EU is toys.

In addition there are specific rules that have arisen from problems discovered during previous product recalls. These include the ban on the sale of novelty cigarette lighters, rules for toys that include magnets, a safety standard for blinds and curtains aimed at eliminating strangulation hazards to young children and a ban on the chemical dimethylfumarate (DMF), a mould-proofing agent from so called 'toxic sofas' that have left people with terrible skin rashes.

There are separate regulations covering food, medicines, medical devices, pharmaceuticals, cosmetics and a range of other non-food products, which come within the remit of various bodies, including the Food Safety Authority of Ireland (for food products) and the Irish Medicines Board (for medical devices, pharmaceuticals and cosmetics), the Health and Safety Authority and the National Standards Authority of Ireland.

The CE Mark
The CE stands for 'Conformité Européenne' (European Conformity) and when you see it on a product or its packaging it indicates that the product is safe. The sign has to be visible and easily readable and can't be rubbed off. There are exact procedures that manufacturers have to follow before affixing the mark.

The mark indicates that:
- The product has been assessed and complies with the essential requirements of relevant product safety legislation.

- It can be legally placed on the market.
- It ensures the free movement for the product within the EU and EFTA countries.
- It permits the withdrawal of the product if it is found not to conform to standards.

RAPEX – Recalls and Enforcement

The RAPEX system is an online rapid alert system for dangerous products, operated by the European Commission under the terms of the General Product Safety Directive.

The aim is to ensure that information is shared among countries about potentially dangerous products with the aim of preventing or restricting the selling of these products on the market. This involves withdrawing them from the EU market and/or recalling them from consumers.

Thirty countries participate in RAPEX: the twenty-seven European Union countries and the EFTA/EEA countries – Iceland, Liechtenstein and Norway.

In January 2006, a Memorandum of Understanding on general product safety was signed between the European Commission Directorate General on Health and Consumer Affairs and the Chinese General Administration for Quality Supervision, Inspection and Quarantine (AQSIQ). One of the measures to come out of this was the development of the RAPEX-China system. This was an important step given that China accounts for 86 per cent of products imported into the EU.

The system in action

Once Member States inform RAPEX about unsafe products found in their country and the measures taken to deal with them, the information is uploaded to the RAPEX database and available for all other countries to see and take relevant action if required. Weekly updates are also compiled and anyone can go online to look at the products that have been notified as unsafe.

In each Member State there is a contact point for sending this information to the Commission to add to the RAPEX system. Here it is the National Consumer Agency (NCA).

When the National Consumer Agency sees an entry that includes Ireland as a distribution destination or finds a potentially dangerous product on sale here, they will get in touch with all product retailers and distributors who stock the product and decide on what action to take.

How a recall works

Product recalls or safety warnings may come from a host of sources:

- Complaints received from consumers via the NCA consumer helpline or from other parties
- Voluntary recalls by manufacturers or distributors in co-operation with the NCA
- Investigation of unsafe products notified by other Member States on RAPEX
- Surveillance activities, often in cooperation with other regulatory bodies in Ireland, e.g. customs authorities
- Joint surveillance initiatives with other Member States

Once a potential safety risk is discovered the most common measures taken are:

- A ban on or halt to sales
- The withdrawal of the dangerous product from the market

- The provision of information to consumers about the risks related to the use of the product

On other occasions, the products may still be in transit to Ireland so Irish consumers will not be affected. If only a few units have been sold, the customers who bought them may be contacted individually. In the case of safety recalls relating to cars, individual owners are generally notified and can be traced through the vehicle registration system if necessary.

Different types of recalls

A product may need to be returned to the retailer for a full refund or brought back for a free repair or part-modification because of potential safety risks. For example, throughout 2010 and into 2011 there were continued calls for owners of particular models of gas cookers to call the manufacturers to arrange a free modification. If the door of the grill was closed while in use there was a risk of carbon monoxide poisoning and a repair was required to rectify the problem.

This is often the case with recalls relating to cars: you bring your car to an authorised dealer for a free modification so that the problem identified can be fixed.

On the other hand, an example of a full recall is when children's hooded jackets were taken off the market: a long drawstring could have caused a choking hazard. Jackets were to be returned to the store where they were purchased for a full refund.

Toy Safety

A new European directive on toy safety came into force in July 2011, replacing legislation that was over twenty years old. It defines toys as 'products designed or intended, whether or not exclusively, for use in play by children under fourteen years of age'.

The law includes:

- Improved rules for the marketing of toys, whether produced or imported into the EU
- Enhanced market surveillance obligations of Member States
- Higher safety requirements that can cope with recently identified hazards

In relation to higher safety requirements, the new law prohibits the use of certain chemicals including carcinogens, reduces the allowed limits of lead and mercury and prohibits allergenic fragrances.

It also bans toys in which a toy is firmly attached to a food product and where food has to be eaten before the child can get to the toy. Toys that are sold with food must now always come in separate packaging with a written warning and cannot present any choking risk.

Information that is required on toys
- The CE mark
- The name and address or trademark of the manufacturer or importer to the EU
- Instruction for use (if required)
- Advice on the safe use of the toy
- If the product has detachable parts it should be marked 'unsuitable for children under 36 months'.
- Any particular hazard that exists should be listed on the packaging.
- A warning sign if there is a magnet in the toy
- Warning signs must be clearly visible, accurate, easily legible and easily understood.

Other things to check for
- Make sure the product is strong and resilient and won't break easily.

- Make sure the product is made of materials that don't burn easily.
- Buy the product from a reputable seller and take extra care if buying at a street market or car boot sale.
- Make sure the toy is suitable for your child's age and pay attention to the 'minimum age' warnings.
- Be particularly careful when buying an electrical toy. Electrical toys with more than 24 volts cannot be sold in Ireland. Make sure the safety instructions are clear and precise.
- If you are buying a bicycle or go-kart there should be adequate brakes and chain-guards. Make sure there is adequate lighting if one is being used on public roads.
- Heed all safety warnings and adopt a commonsense approach.

Who to Complain To

- The National Consumer Agency (NCA) is responsible for enforcing various pieces of product safety legislation. Get in touch with them if you discover an unsafe product or, for example, if you spot a toy without a CE mark: www.consumerconnect.ie/1890-432432/01-4025555.
- If you have suffered loss or damage from using a defective product you should contact the manufacturer of the product who is liable in this case. You may be entitled to damages under legislation governing liability for defective products. You will have to prove your loss, for example personal injury, property damage or financial loss. Be warned that if you have used a product incorrectly it may not have been defective in the first place.

Legislation Name Check

General product safety

Directive 2001/95/EC on general product safety, transposed in Ireland as EC
General Product Safety Regulations 2004. Statutory Instrument No 199 of 2004.

Toy safety

Directive 2009/48/EC on the safety of toys, transposed in Ireland as the EC
Safety of Toys Regulations 2011. Statutory Instrument No 14 of 2011.

10

Food Labelling and Food Safety

Food labelling is a huge area; there are general rules and a host of other rules that apply to specific products such as beef, fish, products with meat as an ingredient, jams, jellies and marmalades, foods containing caffeine, food supplements and alcoholic beverages. In addition there are specific rules for products making nutritional and health claims or for products that may cause allergies, for example gluten-free products and food with additives.

This section covers the main things that you need to know, such as what should be on a label, best before dates and how to check for country of origin.

Food safety is crucial for our health so you should know how food safety is ensured and how you can complain if you get a dodgy tummy after a meal out.

In this Chapter
- What must be on the label
- Country of origin
- 'Buy Irish' labels
- Nutrition labelling
- 'Best before' dates
- Food safety
- Who to complain to
- Legislation name check

What Must Be on the Label
Under general labelling legislation the following must appear on the label:

- Name under which the product is sold*
- List of ingredients
- Quantity of certain ingredients
- Net quantity*
- Date of minimum durability*
- Any special storage instructions or conditions of use
- Name or business name and address of the manufacturer or packager, or of a seller within the European Union
- Place of origin of the foodstuff if its absence might mislead the consumer to a material degree
- Instructions for use where necessary
- Beverages with more than 1.2 per cent alcohol by volume must declare their actual alcoholic strength*

*These details must appear in the same field of vision.

Country of Origin
The above list of what must appear on a label does not stipulate naming the country of origin for all products. In fact, it is compulsory only in two instances: firstly for certain specified food-stuffs and secondly where not to do so would be misleading.

Specified foodstuffs
The specified foodstuffs that must include a country of origin:

- Raw beef and veal
- Raw poultry meat from a third country (i.e. non-EU)
- Fruit and vegetables
- Honey

Labels on these products must follow certain rules. For example the beef has to be born, raised and slaughtered in the country named and fruit and vegetables have to be grown in the country.

But look at the list again: it covers only some raw meat and poultry, which means that ready meals are excluded.

Let us take the example of a chicken dinner. The chicken could be imported from anywhere and then made into a chicken Kiev or chicken nuggets in Ireland. The chicken is no longer raw so even if it comes from a third country the country of origin rule no longer applies.

Having been made into a meal, it has now undergone what's called 'substantive transformation'. An amount of processing has taken place here so while it's not obligatory, the label can now read 'product of Ireland', even though you have no idea where the chicken was reared.

Misleading labels
This is the other scenario where a country of origin must be indicated: let's say a product includes in its name a placename, like Clonakilty black pudding or Parma ham. We assume from the name that the product is from Clonakilty or Parma. But if a product includes a place name just as a marketing gimmick and isn't from that region or country at all, its labelling has to include the country or origin or consumers might otherwise be mislead.

Let's take a fictional product called Wicklow Jam. Perhaps it is just trading on the association with that country as the garden of Ireland but is made somewhere else entirely. In that case the country of origin has to be shown. It can be written quite small on the label – so remember when you are shopping always to take a good look.

New European rules on food labelling are on the way. In July 2011 the European Parliament voted to accept the new rules and the law will come into effect three years after being formally adopted, which should be in 2014.

Compulsory country of origin labelling will be extended to include meat from sheep, goats, poultry and pigs. However, the current rule is that country of origin labelling for other products is voluntary unless its absence would mislead consumers will remain. There will be a minimum allowed size for the font so that it isn't too small to read easily.

It hasn't yet been decided whether the requirements for mandatory country of origin labelling will have to include the specific Member State or just indicate EU origin. It is expected that this will be clarified within the next two years.

Another way of checking where a food product comes from, or at least where it was packed, is by looking at the EU approval number on the packaging. The mark will be an oval with IE, a number and EC written in it. This identifies the final processing plant but does not indicate the origin of the meat or dairy product.

The letters IE indicate that at least some process in the life of the product took place in Ireland. The number equates to a specific approved plant, a list of which you will find on the website of the Department of Agriculture. This information is also handy for finding out if the same manufacturing plant made a supermarket 'own brand' product as a branded household-name product.

'Buy Irish' Labels

If you want to buy Irish but the country of origin is not on the label, you can look out for whether the product carries one of a range of logos indicating it is made in Ireland. These are the main ones:

Bord Bia Quality Assurance Scheme

These logos cover meat, fruit, vegetables and eggs that are 100 per cent Irish. There is also a logo for pre-packed meals containing meat where the meat content is less than 90 per cent. There are four marks: Origin Ireland; Origin Northern Ireland; Produced and Processed in Ireland and Northern Ireland; Origin Ireland Meat Content only.

This label isn't just about being Irish; standards include traceability, animal welfare, environment, safe use of medicines, safe use of chemicals, food safety, hygiene. Members: 40,000 farmers, 150 factories and food production plants audited and certified.

Cost: There is no cost to farmers for the mark. However, one quarter of Bord Bia's funding comes from a levy paid at factory or slaughterhouse level and on live exports. The rest of the body's funding comes from the Department of Agriculture.

National Dairy Council (NDC)

The NDC logo was introduced in September 2009 and is for milk and cream products only, although the intention is to extend it to other dairy products such as cheese, butter and yogurt. The produce must be farmed and processed in Ireland so it is 100 per cent Irish. The mark is approved under licence and audited and 2193 dairy farm families are involved.

Cost: There is a €250 flat fee for administration of the mark and this is paid by the Co-op on behalf of their member farmers. The NDC is funded solely by the farming industry via a levy paid through the Co-ops.

Guaranteed Irish

Established first in 1975 and run by the Irish Goods Council, Guaranteed Irish has been an independent non-profit company since 1984, following a European ruling in 1982 that a state-funded organisation could not promote its own goods over another EU area. The logo covers food products, goods and services, with the criteria that a minimum of 50 per cent of the product/service is manufactured here. There are approximately a thousand members.

Cost: Membership starts at €7 per week (€364 a year) and goes up in multiples of that depending on the size of the company and type of use of the logo. This is the sole income of the company.

Love Irish Food
Established in September 2009, this logo covers food products only. To fulfill the logo's criteria a minimum of 80 per cent of brand revenue must be derived from a Republic of Ireland manufacturing process. Primary ingredients must be sourced from Ireland where possible, with some exceptions, such as tea and cocoa beans for example, or food that is seasonally unavailable. There are currently approximately eighty members.

Cost: From €1000 up to €30,000 per year; the cost depends on the size and turnover of the business. This is the sole income for the company.

Nutrition Labelling
If you are watching your weight or care about how much salt you are eating, the chances are you'll check out the nutritional values provided on the product's packaging. You do see clear nutritional information on most products. However, this is mainly voluntary on the part of the manufacturer and is a clear response to what consumers want.

It is not compulsory for all products to include nutrition labelling. In fact it is currently compulsory only if a nutritional claim is made on the label, for example that the product is high in fibre or low in fat. Then the label must comply with regulations and include the following information:

- Energy value

- Nutrients (protein, carbohydrate, fat, fibre sodium and components of them)
- Certain vitamins and minerals, if present in significant amounts

The rules also prescribe the claims that can and cannot be made in relation to nutrition and health. In addition any such claims must be clear and accurate and based on scientific evidence.

New European rules on nutrition labelling are on the way. In July 2011 the European Parliament voted to accept the new rules and the law will come into effect three years after being formally adopted, so we should have them by 2014. Information on nutritional composition (energy, fat, saturated fat, carbohydrate, sugar, protein and salt), will be mandatory for food labels, as will information on allergens. This will have to be shown in a minimum size and font so it is easier to read.

However, not all the rules put forward by the European Commission were accepted so it has stated that it thinks the new rules don't go far enough. For example, the proposal for nutrition labelling on the front of packages was not accepted and the European Parliament made the decision to exempt alcoholic drinks from the ingredient and nutrition labelling requirements.

'Best Before' Dates
There are dates other than 'best before' dates on food items but for convenience we can use this heading as a catch-all.

Under current food labelling legislation, it is mandatory to include a product's shelf-life or 'date of minimum durability' on the label and this information must be in the same field of vision as the name of the foodstuff and the net quantity. Even in exceptional cases in which a date of minimum durability is not required by law it is considered best practice to include it.

Rather than being an indication of safety, a 'best before' date is one of quality. After the 'best before' date, you can expect the taste of the food to deteriorate but it won't kill you. A 'best-before' date is not defined under law but can be described as the date up until which a food can reasonably be expected to retain its optimum conditions, that is when it comes to the specific properties that are normally associated with that food. Examples of foods that fall into this category include frozen, canned and dried foods.

You can adopt a commonsense approach when it comes to eating this food (use your eyes and nose). Nutritionists say that the food will have a 'compromised nutritional value' when it is well beyond the date. For example, levels of Vitamin B in rice may not be as high if the rice is very old and grubs will appear in flour if it is not stored in an airtight container.

Sell by/display until dates
Other dates on food might include a 'sell by' date or a 'display until' date. These are primarily to assist with stock control. They are not legal terms and do not relate to the safety of the item.

'Use-by' dates
This is the crucial one. The 'use-by' date is required by law on foods that are highly perishable, as they could pose a danger to health once they go off. Most fresh, ready-to-eat and chilled foods fall into this category. The advice is that such food cannot be consumed, cooked or processed safely after the 'use by' date.

EU law states that food must not be placed on the market if it is unsafe. Unsafe food is defined as being: a) injurious to health; and b) unfit for human consumption. As foodstuffs that are past their 'use-by' date could be unsafe due to possible deterioration and the risk of illness if they are consumed, it is illegal to sell them.

Eggs

The one food where a 'best before' date rather than a 'use-by' date is legally required is on eggs. This is called the date of minimum durability which has to be no more than twenty-eight days after laying. European legislation also requires that eggs are stored, transported and marketed in a way that aims to maintain as constant a temperature as possible. This is current practice within the industry and the reason why the majority of retail outlets stock eggs on shelves rather than in fridges. This is because if you take the egg from a fridge, take it out to bring it home, then put it back in a fridge once you arrive home, this could lead to condensation forming on an eggshell which could cause the growth of mould as well as the possibility that bacteria might infect the eggs as a result.

You are advised to refrigerate eggs as soon as possible after purchase to maintain their freshness and reduce the possibility of bacteria growth resulting from any exposure to temperature and humidity variations in the home kitchen. Also beware of cracks or damage to the shell as bacteria can get in this way. Pregnant women, babies and toddlers are advised not to eat runny yolks.

Food Safety

When it comes to food safety and hygiene any business serving food has to comply with the relevant law and guidelines. Anyone running a restaurant, café, deli, canteen, food stall or serving food has to adhere to a great deal of regulation.

Aside from general hygiene and safety, there are rules about food preparation, food storage and the temperatures at which it is stored. Staff training is mandatory to make sure that anyone handling food, whether in a top-end restaurant or at a deli counter, understands and follows the safety rules.

For example, a system called Hazard Analysis & Critical Control Point (HACCP) allows the business to identify and control any hazards that could pose a danger to the preparation of safe food. It involves identifying what can go wrong, planning to prevent it and making sure you are doing it. HACCP is a legal requirement.

How food safety is enforced

The Food Safety Authority of Ireland (FSAI) is responsible for enforcing food safety legislation in Ireland and one of the pieces of legislation that gives it its enforcement powers is the Food Safety of Ireland Act 1998. The FSAI covers all food items sold in any shop, food producers, manufacturers, distributors, restaurants and other retail premises preparing and selling cooked and prepared food.

The role of the FSAI covers a multitude: monitoring and enforcement, including carrying out national food alerts (if a potential food risk is associated with a particular product); programmes with manufacturers on nutrition and health such as the salt-reduction programme; training and seminars; surveillance of foods that have been modified either genetically or chemically; checking labelling and more.

Inspections/enforcements

In association with FSAI, inspections are carried out mainly by Health Services Executive (HSE) staff but also by the Sea Fisheries Protection Agency, the Department of Agriculture and local authorities, with food businesses categorised by risk. Depending on the situation, different enforcement actions may occur:

- An improvement notice can be issued if the premises or practice poses or is likely to pose a risk to public health.
- If the improvement notice is not complied with, an improvement order can be issued by the district court.
- A closure order can be issued if there is likely to be grave and immediate danger to public health. Closures orders can refer to the immediate closure of all or part of the food premises, or all or some of its activities. The orders may be lifted when the premises has improved to the satisfaction of the authorised

officer. Failure to comply with an improvement order may result in the issuing of a closure order.

- A prohibition order can also be issued if any activity that could come from a particular product or batch or item of food is likely to involve a serious risk to public health. This order will prohibit the sale of a particular product, either temporarily or permanently.

All orders are listed in a database on the FSAI website for everyone to see (www.fsai.ie). Closure and improvement orders remain in this database for a period of three months from the date the order was lifted. Prohibition orders remain in the database for a period of one month from the date the order was lifted.

Who to Complain To

The Food Safety Authority of Ireland (FSAI) is responsible for ensuring that food labelling laws are complied with. You can also get in touch with them if you notice dirt or bad hygiene in a premises serving food or if you get sick after a meal out. In such a case the FSAI will liaise with the HSE in that area to ensure the premises is inspected: www.fsai.ie/1890-336677.

Safefood is an all-Ireland body tasked with the job of promoting, informing and raising awareness about issues relating to food safety and also engaging in research and surveillance: www.safefood. ie/1850-404 567/021 2304100/01-4480600.

Legislation Name Check

Food labelling
EC Directive 2000/13/EC: European Communities (Labelling, Presentation and Advertising of Foodstuffs) Regulations 2002, transposed to Irish law by Statutory Instrument No 483 of 2002.

This Directive was subsequently amended by EC Directive 2001/101/EC regulating the definition of meat for labelling purposes and by EC Directive 2003/89/EC regarding the indication of ingredients present in foodstuffs. Further, EC Directive 2003/89 EC clarifies some questions relating to the indication of the ingredients listed in Annex IIIa of the Directive 2000/13/EC and Directive 2005/26/EC establishes a list of substances provisionally exempted. Commission Directive 2006/142/EC provides for a further amendment and lists the ingredients which must under all circumstances appear on the labelling of foodstuffs; Commission Directive 2007/68/EC further amends the Directive regarding certain foodstuffs and Commission Directive 2008/5/EC contains amendments concerning the compulsory indication on the labelling.

Statutory Instruments transposing the various amendments are: SI No 228 of 2005, SI No 647 of 2005, SI No 808 of 2007, SI No 424 of 2008 and SI No 61 of 2009.

Food safety

Food Safety Authority of Ireland Act, 1998. Statutory Instrument No 540 of 1998.

11

Air Passenger Rights

It's not exotic any longer, nor is it always a comfortable or even an enjoyable experience, but thanks to low-cost airlines air travel is something we now take for granted. Flying from Cork to Dublin can be as handy as getting the train and flying anywhere really isn't a big deal any longer. But can things go wrong? Of course they can. If your luggage has been lost, your flight delayed or worse or if you've ever been stranded anywhere, you'll know all about it. And it's at times like this that you'll need to know your rights as an air passengers.

In this Chapter
- Delayed flights
- Cancelled flights
- Denied boarding
- Lost, damaged or delayed luggage
- Airfare display rules
- Who to complain to
- Legislation name check

Delayed Flights
The relevant legislation lays out the hours that must pass before your rights in respect of a delayed flight kick in:

- Delays of two hours or more in the case of flights of 1500km or less
- Delays of three hours or more in the case of all intra-EU flights of more than 1500km and of all other flights of

between 1500 and 3500km

- Delays of four hours or more in the case of all other flights

If your flight is delayed past these timeframes, you should receive care and assistance. This means:

- Meals and refreshments in reasonable relation to the waiting time
- Two telephone calls, faxes or emails
- Hotel accommodation when a stay of one or more nights becomes necessary
- Transport between the airport and the place of accommodation

If your flight is delayed by five hours or more and you decide not to travel, you are entitled to a refund for the part or parts of the journey not completed. If you accept the refund, you are not entitled to any further care from the air carrier, such as meals or accommodation.

Financial compensation for delays

The law that covers this area doesn't allow for additional financial compensation for delays. However, in 2010 the European Court of Justice delivered a ruling (in the cases of Sturgeon-v- Condor Flugdienst GmbH and Bock and Others-v- Air France; SA C-402/2007 and C-432/2007) that financial compensation should be payable in delay situations. There were provisos attached to this ruling. Firstly you have to reach your destination three or more hours after the original scheduled time. Secondly if the delay is caused by extraordinary circumstances, which could not be avoided if all reasonable measures were taken, you won't be entitled to it.

There is a piece of international legislation, the Montreal Convention, that allows for compensation for damages arising from delayed flights but this also includes the extraordinary circumstances opt-out.

Cancelled Flights

The same European law applies here: if your flight is cancelled you can choose between three options:

- Wait to be put on the next available flight
- Reschedule for a later date
- Get a full refund and find your own way home

In the first scenario, if you choose to wait for the next available flight, the airline is obliged to provide you with care and assistance:

- Meals and refreshments in reasonable relation to the waiting time
- Two telephone calls, faxes or emails
- Hotel accommodation where a stay of one or more nights becomes necessary
- Transport between the airport and the place of accommodation

This care should be offered to you straight away rather than your paying yourself and having to apply for reimbursement afterwards. That way you shouldn't be out of pocket or find yourself having to worry about how to pay for a hotel room.

But who can forget the disruption caused by air traffic strikes, snow and most of all the volcanic ash cloud in 2010.

In that unprecedented situation, when air space around Europe was closed for long periods, many travellers found themselves forking out for rooms and meals. If you ever find yourself in this situation, be sure to keep your receipts and submit them to the airline for reimbursement.

The legislation does not specify which grade of accommodation or meals should be offered but during the ash cloud crisis, the European Commission came out and said that expenses should be 'reasonable' – which, needless to say, is open to interpretation.

What about additional financial compensation?

If a flight is cancelled you are entitled to financial compensation of between €250 and €600 depending on the length of the flight: for example, €250 for flights of 1500km and less; €400 for flights between 1500km and 3500km and €600 for all other flights.

Don't get too excited, though, because in practice this compensation isn't given very often. Here's why:

The carrier does not have to offer compensation in relation to a cancelled flight if you have been informed of the cancellation two weeks in advance of the departure date. Or if you were informed seven days before departure and the rescheduled flight's arrival is less that four hours late, or within seven days if the rescheduled flight is less than two hours late at its final destination.

But to make matters even more complicated, an airline is not liable to pay compensation for any cancellation if they have done everything they can to avoid it.

It's worth reproducing the relevant paragraph of the law to make this clear: '*An operating air carrier shall not be obliged to pay compensation...if it can prove that the cancellation is caused by extraordinary circumstances which could not have been avoided even if all reasonable measures had been taken.*'

Unfortunately the meaning of 'extraordinary circumstances' is not defined in the legislation. However, there is an explanatory note to the regulation which offers the following examples:

- Political instability
- Bad weather
- Security risk
- Unexpected flight risk

- Strikes

Bear in mind that while strikes and bad weather are listed here, we cannot assume that this applies to each and every flight that is cancelled during a period of industrial dispute or bad weather.

The airline is exempt from providing financial compensation only if they can prove that they took all 'reasonable measures' to avoid the cancellation. In practice it may be the case that flights are sometimes cancelled to facilitate schedule changes: proving this is another matter.

EU air passenger rights cover all flights departing from an EU/EEA country and also those arriving into an EU/EEA country from a non-EU country on an EU licensed carrier, that is unless assistance was already received under the third country's rules.

Denied Boarding
If there are health, safety or security concerns, if you don't have the correct travel documents or if you arrive too late for check-in or boarding, the airline may have reasonable grounds to deny you boarding and you'll be owed nothing.

However, flights can be overbooked and in this case you most certainly have specific rights. This is what should happen:

- The air carrier must call on passengers to volunteer their seats to other passengers.
- If a volunteer comes forward they are entitled to a sum of money in compensation, which should be agreed between the airline and the volunteer.
- The volunteer can also choose between an alternative flight or a refund.

If no volunteer comes forward, you hope you won't be the one bumped off the flight against your will but the airline can do it. If they do, you can choose between being rerouted (say on the next flight), or a refund for the part or parts of the journey you haven't made yet.

If you choose to wait to be rerouted, just as in the case of delay or cancellation you are entitled to care, including meals and refreshments and hotel accommodation if necessary. In addition, you are entitled to financial compensation and the airline can't avoid paying this. You should get:

- €250 per passenger for flights of 1500km or less
- €400 per passenger for intra-EU flights of more than 1500km and for other flights between 1500km and 3500km
- €600 per passenger for all other flights

Airlines are supposed to tell you all this. They have an obligation to inform passengers of their rights. Firstly they should have a notice at check-in with specific text advising passengers: 'if you are denied boarding or if your flight is cancelled or delayed for at least two hours, ask at the check-in counter or boarding gate for the text stating your rights, particularly with regard to compensation and assistance.'

In case of cancellation or delay that text to be provided is a written notice with details of the rules for assistance and compensation, plus info on the enforcement agency responsible.

If you don't get the information in these circumstances, ask for it.

Lost, Damaged or Delayed Luggage

Most people think that if their luggage goes missing their only option is to claim under your travel insurance. You can do this, if you have insurance and your policy covers it, but you do have consumer rights in this area. The Montreal Convention entitles you to compensation for lost bags and also for bags that are delayed or damaged.

How much can you get?

If your luggage is lost, damaged or delayed you can claim up to 1131 SDR (Special Drawing Rights), which is approximately €1275.

(An 'SDR' is based on a basket of international currencies. The conversion rate changes every day and the calculation is made by the International Monetary Fund. You can find it on www.imf.org).

You cannot claim more than this under Montreal, no matter what the value of your contents. In practice airlines generally offer well below this upper liability limit.

Timeframes

There are strict timeframes for claiming provided in the legislation:

- Damaged luggage: within seven days
- Delayed luggage: within twenty-one days
- Lost luggage: deemed lost after twenty-one days or if the airline admits loss

Your complaint should be made in writing, not verbally. A big mistake is that passengers think that filling out the Property Irregularity Report (PIR form) at the airport constitutes a complaint. It doesn't. By filling the PIR form you are identifying your missing bag to the airline and asking them to search for it or you are reporting damage.

To claim for compensation you must write to the airline within the prescribed timeframe. Include a copy of the PIR, luggage tags, evidence of damage if this is the case and receipts for necessary expenditure.

Remember, the maximum amount of compensation is not automatically payable. In fact it may be up to you to prove the extent of the loss: this is where your problems can begin:

- The Montreal convention doesn't provide guidelines on how to calculate the amount of compensation to be awarded in each individual case.
- In practice many airlines insist on receipts. This is fine if your luggage was delayed and you are simply claiming for the clothes and toothbrush you needed to buy while waiting for your luggage to arrive. However, if your bag has been lost, you won't have receipts for all the contents. You could seek old credit card statements for some items, for example, but you still probably won't be able to provide them all. Remember, just submitting the cost of replacement items when your luggage has been lost won't do: you have to prove the cost of the actual loss, not the replacement. Even if receipts are produced, many airlines refuse to pay the full price of replacing items and, instead, take money off for 'depreciation' and 'wear and tear'.
- Some airlines don't seek receipts and others use the method used by the loss assessors of insurance companies and treat the lost bags as cargo and compensate per kilo. In this case they sometimes go by the provisions of the Warsaw Convention (the predecessor of the Montreal Convention), which allows 17 SDRs per Kilo. So you could get €300-€350 for the total bag.

By the way, if you make a claim for lost luggage to your travel insurer they will need you to submit proof of the loss and receipts or credit card statements. This should be made clear in your policy.

The lesson from all this is that you should never place valuable items such as cameras, jewellery, money and laptops in your checked-in luggage. Most airlines advise this on their websites. You could also consider making a 'Special Declaration of Interest' at the airport. This is like buying insurance: for a fee, you can declare to the airline that you are checking in goods of a particular value. You will have the right to a higher compensation amount than normal in this case if something goes wrong.

Be aware that there are strict time limits on claiming compensation and sometimes you have to find receipts to prove your loss.

Airfare Display Rules

When it comes to the display of airfares on the internet the price you
see should be the price you pay; that is before any optional 'extras'
are taken into account. Airlines are legally obliged to provide an
'all-inclusive' final price at the beginning of the booking process
and a breakdown of this final inclusive price. It should include the
fare or rate, the taxes, airport charges and any other charges that
are 'unavoidable'. This law has been in place since November 2008,
which is why you now see the final price displayed at the start of the
booking process and the breakdown of what the fare consists of.

However, as the legislation specifies that this final price must
include only 'unavoidable' charges, it leaves plenty of scope for
airlines to add a host of optional extras later in the booking process.
These optional extras could be such things as checked-in luggage,
priority boarding and seat choice.

This is also why both Ryanair and Aer Lingus always offer their
customers the choice of using one particular card on which they
won't levy a booking or administration fee. After all, if all cards
attracted a fee, this would not be an optional cost and that €12
return would have to be added to the final price that is shown up
front.

The regulation also outlaws having to opt out of services such as
insurance by way of ticking a box. Instead you should always have to
opt in if choosing to buy any extra product or service.

Getting your unused taxes and charges back

When you buy a flight ticket it includes taxes and charges such as government taxes, airport charges, insurance charges, security fees and a wheelchair levy. If you have to cancel your flight you will most likely not be allowed a refund of the cost of the fare (this depends on the terms and conditions) but the taxes and charges will not have to be passed on to the relevant government or airport authority and this means that you are entitled to get them back.

However, in Ireland both Ryanair and Aer Lingus impose strict timeframes and charge administration fees for issuing these refunds. In addition the airline may allow you to request only some of the charges back. Once you deduct the fee from what you are owed it may be that you will get nothing at all or very little, thus making it not worth your while.

In 2010 an Irish website, www.airtaxrefund.com, was launched to campaign against this practice. For a small fee (a percentage of the recovered charges) they will also assist you in getting back your unused taxes and charges.

Mobility for Air Passengers

Under an EU regulation that came into force in 2008, all airports and airlines have to provide free services to people with disabilities and reduced mobility. The regulation allows for the airport management to charge the airline based on true costs and specifies that this is not to be a profit-making exercise. You will find that a small charge for this service is usually passed on to all passengers within the 'taxes and charges'.

Your main entitlements

- An air carrier cannot refuse carriage on grounds of disability or reduced mobility.
- You have a right to assistance if departing, arriving or transiting through an EU airport on a commercial air service

and if you're arriving in the EU from an airport outside the EU as long as the airline is an EU-licensed carrier.

- You should inform your airline that you require assistance at least forty-eight hours in advance of travel.
- Assistance should be free of charge.
- Assistance to be provided includes transiting through an airport as well as embarking on and disembarking from a plane.
- You should present yourself at one of the designated points of arrival at the airport, details of which you should find on every airport's website.
- If either the airport or the airline loses or damages wheelchairs, mobility equipment or assistive devices you are entitled to compensation. The compensation is as per levels set under the Montreal Convention (see lost luggage above).

Who to Complain To

Whatever your complaint you should always complain to the airline first and try to resolve it that way. If this doesn't work here's what you can do:

For complaints about delayed or cancelled flights, denied boarding and mobility assistance

- The Commission for Aviation Regulation (CAR) enforces the legislation that governs these areas and has a complaints process for passengers. Confusingly, the law prescribes that the regulator in the country where the incident has occurred is responsible for handling the complaint. This means that if your flight was cancelled in Germany, CAR has to forward your complaint to their German equivalent, who will then correspond directly with you. Bear in mind that these are enforcement bodies: that is to say their job is to ensure that airlines comply with the law. So their primary motive is not to get refunds for passengers. However, CAR will examine every complaint on a case-by-case basis to determine if the law has been broken: CAR: www.aviationreg.ie/01-6611700.

- You can always use the small claims procedure, whether against an Irish airline or one from another EU country. See Chapter 18 for more information: www.courts.ie or phone the district court closest to the airline's registered address.

For complaints about lost, damaged or delayed luggage

- This area isn't governed by any enforcement body so you'll have to take a small claims action if you can't resolve your complaint directly with the airline: www.courts.ie or phone the district court closest to the airline's registered address.
- Alternatively, if your complaint about luggage is against an airline from another EU country you can turn to the European Consumer Centre, as it assists with cross-border consumer disputes: www.eccireland.ie/01-8797620.

For complaints relating to the display of airfares

Under the 2008 legislation governing this an 'authorised officer' should be appointed to enforce Article 23 (the section that deals with air fare display). In Ireland none has as yet been appointed. In the meantime contact either the NCA or CAR.

Legislation Name Check

Cancelled and delayed flights, denied boarding

Regulation (EC) No 261/2004: establishing common rules on compensation and assistance to passengers in the event of denied boarding or of cancellation or long delay of flights.

Lost, damaged and delayed luggage and delayed flights

Montreal Convention 1999 for the unification of certain rules for international carriage by air.

Airfare display

Regulation (EC) No 1008/2008 on common rules for the operation of air services in the European Community.

Mobility for air passengers

Regulation (EC) No 1107/2006) concerning the rights of disabled persons and persons with reduced mobility when travelling by air.

12

Package Holidays

The south of Spain, Portugal of France? An apartment by the sea, a fancy hotel or self-catering? Or how about a guided tour of Egypt's historical sites or a cruise around the Mediterranean?

You can spend hours poring over holiday brochures or browsing agents' offerings online and the good news is that if you opt for a package holiday you are well protected by consumer legislation.

In this Chapter:
- What is a package holiday?
- Package holiday rights
- When something goes wrong before you travel
- When something goes wrong on arrival
- Package holidays versus dynamic holidays
- Who to complain to
- Legislation name check

What is a Package Holiday?
A package holiday is defined by law as a holiday that has been prearranged and sold to you at an inclusive price, either by a travel agent or a tour operator. It should cover at least twenty-four hours (or include an overnight stay) and has to be made up of at least two of the following components: transport; accommodation; and other tourist services such as guided tours.

It doesn't matter if you pay separately for the different elements:

the crucial thing is that you have one contract for all the services provided in the package. However, if extra arrangements are made specifically for you on request, these are not regarded as part of the package.

Package Holiday Rights

The first thing you will read is the brochure, whether in print or online, which describes the holiday to you. Your decision to buy a holiday is based on this information so the legislation insists that all information provided should be accurate and should not be misleading.

In effect the information provided forms the terms of your contract and these terms are binding on the agent or operator. In other words if you are advised that a hotel is child-friendly and on the beach or that meals are included, that is exactly what you should get.

By law the following information must be provided in the brochure:
- Destination and dates
- Transportation arrangements
- Type, location and description of accommodation
- Itinerary and meal plan
- Price and payment terms
- Any tax or compulsory charges
- Other essential information including passport and visa requirements and health formalities
- The deadline for informing consumers in the event of cancellation

When Something Goes Wrong before You Travel

Let's say it is a few weeks before departure and your agent or tour operator contacts you to say that the hotel you booked is no longer available and that you'll have to stay in another resort. That's not on, as they are changing the terms of the contract you have agreed to. So the legislation gives you three choices:

1. A replacement package of equivalent or superior quality
2. A lower grade package and to recover the difference in price between the two
3. A full refund

Nor is it, in general, permissible for the tour operator to get in touch with you to tell you that the price has changed (and it is inevitably to tell you that it has gone up). If this happens you have the same three choices as above. However, there are specific instances where a price change is allowed: for example if there are significant currency fluctuations, changes to government tax or duty or variations in the price of fuel. With the price of fuel still rising, this is one to watch out for. But even if you are asked to pay more and are specifically given fuel price increases as the reason, the price cannot change within twenty days of departure.

When Something Goes Wrong on Arrival

It's only when you arrive, tired and excited, sun screen in your bag and flip flops on your feet, that you will know whether all that information that led you to choose the holiday in the first place was accurate and true. Everyone knows someone who has had a holiday from hell at one time or other.

There are the hotels that turn out to be five miles from the beach rather than five hundred metres; so called child-friendly accommodation with steep concrete steps and no railings around the pool; promised excursions and free meals that never materialise; one small room stuffed with four beds rather than the two double rooms booked; a building site next door offering a new dimension to the peaceful and quiet holiday promised; dirty rooms and even urine-stained sheets.

These are among the stories I have heard and no doubt there are plenty more. The question is: what can you do about it?

Remember that information you were given in the brochure, with the description of the accommodation and activities? If what you get isn't what you signed up for, the agent or tour operator has broken their contract with you and this needs to be remedied.

The first thing you should do is to seek out the holiday company representative or organiser and try to resolve the problem. This could involve moving rooms or going to another hotel and you shouldn't have to pay extra. Make sure you fill out a complaint form (the reps should have one), as that will come in handy as proof that you tried to sort things out, if the worst happens and nothing is sorted for you.

In that case, take photos or video of anything that is amiss. This will form part of your evidence if you have to complain when you get home. If you do have to complain when you arrive home, don't delay. The legislation prescribes that you have to complain in writing with twenty-eight days of your return.

If the problems were not sorted, you are entitled to compensation. Calculating how much you deserve will be up to you, as that is not detailed in the legislation.

A useful exercise is to take the total cost of your holiday and divide it by the number of days you spent on it. Now you have a daily cost, work out how much time and money you lost due to the discrepancies between what you booked and what you experienced on the ground. Basically you are seeking damages for the untrue information that was given to you.

When you arrive at what you think you deserve in compensation ask for that clearly in your letter of complaint. Don't be greedy; you cannot generally expect a full refund. After all, you *have* had a holiday; it is just that not all of it was what you expected.

The travel agent or tour operator may respond by saying they can't offer you anything or by offering a paltry sum. You can accept that or you can take it further (small claims or arbitration) so check the terms and conditions to see what complaints procedure the holiday company has in place.

Package holidays – the safest way to book?
Are package holidays the safest way to go? If you're talking about not losing money, the answer is yes.

This is because travel agents and tour operators must be licensed by the Commission for Aviation Regulation (CAR) to operate in Ireland. They pay a percentage of sales into a bond run by CAR. The bond will pay out if the company goes bust and your holiday is cancelled, or if you are stranded abroad it will fly you home. There is no similar scheme for airlines or hotels, which makes the package holiday a safer bet.

This was obvious when airports closed during the ash cloud crisis of 2010. If you had booked a flight and accommodation separately, you could get a refund for the cancelled flight but not for the accommodation. However, if you had a booked a package holiday, both flight and accommodation could be refunded or rearranged for a later date so you wouldn't have lost any hard-earned cash.

Package Holidays versus Dynamic Holidays

I have described what package holidays are and the consumer protection you have when you book them. But now there are many online agents who sell 'dynamic packages', and this can be very confusing for consumers.

Their offer is something along the lines of: 'Why go on a holiday that we have chosen for you when you can choose your own?' They allow you to choose your own holiday components rather than having to go along with a package they have put together.

This may look and seem like a regulated package holiday but it is not. Components such as hotel accommodation, flights and transfers are purchased at individual prices, often from different service-providers. Therefore, it is not covered by package holiday legislation, as under that legislation a package holiday is one that has been prearranged by the seller.

Essentially the agent is arranging and supplying the services. But your contract for the performance of the service will be with the provider of the service: for example, directly with the airline or hotel.

There is absolutely nothing wrong with booking your holiday this way and the sellers aren't doing anything wrong either but just be aware that you are not entitled to the same legal protection as you would when booking a package:

- You won't be able to submit a complaint to the agent but will have to contact each service-provider directly.
- You are not protected by the rules of package holiday legislation.
- The price you pay to the agent may not be the final price if extras are charged later by, for example, a low-cost airline. With a package holiday the price cannot change, except under certain specified conditions.
- Suppliers of regulated package holidays ensure that the services are supplied to a reasonable standard (for instance, by checking hotels) but there is no requirement for providers of dynamic packages to do this.
- If the flight is cancelled by industrial action or adverse weather conditions, you could lose the money you paid for your accommodation; this wouldn't happen if it was a package holiday.

More protection required

Package holidays were once how most of us booked our week in the sun. Not any longer, given the rise of low-fare airlines and the ease of booking accommodation directly online, either yourself or via a 'dynamic package' agent. But legislation has not yet caught up with our change in habits. The EU directive governing package holidays dates from the early 1990s, before the internet turned us all into travel agents.

This is set to change with new EU package holidays legislation in the pipeline. Two areas being examined carefully by this review reflect the changed holiday landscape: how to protect travellers in the case of airline insolvency and how to protect consumers who book the various components of their holiday themselves or book dynamic holidays.

This will all take time. Once the updated legislation is agreed – which may be in 2011 – and then officially published, it will be another few years before it comes into force around Europe.

Who to Complain To

Always complain to the travel agent or tour operator first. If the organiser refuses to offer any compensation you can pursue the matter through the small claims procedure. This will cost you €18 and you can claim up to €2000: www.courts.ie.

An alternative is arbitration: this may be offered as the procedure for dealing with complaints in the terms and conditions of your contract. In arbitration an independent third party makes a decision after considering all the relevant information in the dispute. The decision can either be binding or non-binding, depending on the terms of the arbitration agreement. In arbitration you will be able to claim more than you would in the small claims procedure but it may cost you more. The Chartered Institute of Arbitrators runs a scheme for consumers with travel industry disputes: www.arbitration.ie.

If your complaint is against a travel agent or tour operator based in another European country, you can turn to Ireland's European Consumer Centre (ECC) for assistance as they deal with cross-border consumer disputes: www.eccireland.ie/01-8797620.

For further information on licensed and bonded travel agents and tour operators go to the Commission for Aviation Regulation: www.aviationreg.ie.

Legislation Name Check

The Package Holidays and Travel Trade Act 1995 gives effect to Council Directive No 90/314/EEC on package travel, package holidays and package tours.

13

Train and Taxi Rights

Just as when travelling by air, you have rights when travelling by train. EU legislation for passenger rights on buses and ferries is on the way. When it comes to rail passenger rights, although they are modelled on air passenger rights and bring together the various components such as delay, cancellation, luggage and accessibility, they are not as strong as your rights as an airline passenger.

In addition one thing air passenger rights legislation does not do is differentiate between domestic and cross-border travel. Unfortunately, the law relating to train travel does. It allows for a temporary exemption (up to fifteen years) for domestic rail passenger services in relation to key aspects of the legislation that relate to compensation. The Irish government has chosen to opt for this exemption.

That means that in Ireland the full provisions of the legislation apply only to the Dublin-Belfast route, as that's the only cross-border service we have.

In this Chapter
- General protection
- Rights on cross-border train services
- Taxis
- Who to complain to
- Legislation name check

General Protection

The following rules apply to all train services, cross-border, domestic, urban, suburban and regional:

- Tickets must be made available via ticket offices, vending machines and on board trains, along with adequate provision of information.
- The rail company is liable for loss or damage resulting from the death, personal injury or other physical or mental harm to a passenger (unless it's the passenger's fault or it's the fault of a third party but not another rail company using the same railway infrastructure).
- The rail company has to cover necessary costs: for example, transport, funeral costs in the case of death and costs including treatment and transport in the case of injury as well as compensation due to total or partial incapacity to work.
- The amount of damages should be determined in accordance with national laws. But the regulation states that the upper limit per passenger is set at 175,000 units (€206,500) for incapacity compensation or compensation for people left unsupported by the death ('persons whom the passenger had a legal duty to maintain').
- For lost luggage in general, the rail company is liable up to 1200 units (approximately €1416) but not if it is under the passenger's own care and supervision. As Iarnród Éireann/ Irish Rail does not provide a registered luggage system, your luggage is always in your care so this clause won't apply, unless you can prove that the carrier caused the damage in some way.
- Reservations and tickets have to be offered to disabled persons and those with reduced mobility at no additional cost.
- Upon request, disabled persons and persons with reduced mobility must be provided with information about the accessibility of rail services, about the access conditions of rolling stock and about the facilities on board.
- Adequate measures must be taken to ensure passengers' personal security in railway stations and on trains.

In relation to passengers with reduced mobility Iarnród Éireann/ Irish Rail employs a dedicated accessibility officer, provide information and an accessibility guide and operate a disability user group. This group comprises: National Council for the Blind; Deafhear.ie; National Council of Ageing and Older People; and National Guide Dogs for the Blind. Iarnród Éireann aims for all services to be fully accessible by 2015.

Rights on Cross-border Train Services

There are some minor rules such as the railway having to allow passengers to bring bicycles on board, assuming the train can allow it. But the biggest are the compensation rules laid down for delayed and cancelled trains.

These rules apply to cross-border train services in other EU countries but in Ireland only to the Dublin-Belfast route.

Reimbursement or rerouting

If a delay is more than a hour, you can choose to be reimbursed for the full cost of the ticket as well as getting a return service to the point of departure, or you may choose to continue or reroute either at the earliest opportunity or at a later date suitable to you.

Compensation (if not reimbursed)

25 per cent of the ticket price (one way) for sixty-minute to 119 minute delay; 50 per cent of the ticket price (one way) for a delay of two hours or more. The compensation is to be paid within a month of the passenger's request for it and can be given in vouchers or money, whichever the passenger prefers. However, the compensation cannot be reduced by fees, telephone costs or the price of stamps.

A minimum threshold can be introduced under which compensation will not be paid but this can't be less than €4.

You are not entitled to compensation if you were told of the delay before you bought the ticket or if the delay is less than sixty minutes. Furthermore, the carrier is not liable for compensation if the delay or cancellation was due to circumstances not connected with the operation of the railway.

Assistance

If the delay is more than sixty minutes you have to get: meals and refreshments if they can be reasonably supplied; hotel accommodation and transport to and from it if required; alternative transport to final destination if required.

> Note that Iarnród Éireann/Irish Rail has a Passenger's Charter that can be checked and used if something goes wrong on any rail service. The charter does not affect passengers' legal rights or obligations and therefore the two systems are compatible. Although the legislation does not cover compensation in the case of delay or cancellation on domestic services, Iarnród Éireann/Irish Rail does operate a compensation system, mainly paid in vouchers.

Taxis

The National Transport Authority (NTA) is responsible for the regulation of taxis. Specifically, the Taxi Regulation Directorate, which is within the NTA, carries out the management and administration of taxi regulation.

Taxi fares, including any 'add-ons', are set and there are rules to which all taxi drivers have to adhere. Enforcement (or compliance) officers, who work with the Gardaí and can also work with the Revenue Commissioners, have the authority to issue fines and apply penalty points when the rules have been breached.

A fixed charge (currently €250) can be issued when an offence occurs or a driver can be prosecuted for offences including: not having a driver's or vehicle licence; overcharging; failing to comply with taxi-meter rules; and plying for hire at a point other than a stand.

Complaints

The Taxi Regulation Directorate of the National Transport Authority runs an official complaints procedure for consumers: www.taxiregulation.nationaltransport.ie/076-1064000. You can fill in an online complaint form via the website or you can telephone and request that a form be sent to you by post.

But under the legislation the regulator can hear complaints only about specific things. These are:

- The condition and cleanliness of the vehicle
- The conduct or behaviour of an SPSV (small public service vehicle) operator or driver
- Overcharging and other matters related to fares
- The hiring of an SPSV

If the complaint relates to a criminal matter, such as licensing, it is a matter for An Garda Síochána.

The Taxi Regulator will not process complaints submitted anonymously and if the complaint leads to prosecution you may have to appear in court.

- If you have to make a complaint the crucial thing is that you have the details of the taxi vehicle and the best way of getting these is to get a receipt. If you ask for one the driver is legally obliged to give it to you and the receipt will contain the following information: the taxi licence number; registration number; the date, start time and end time of the journey; breakdown of fare and total charged.
- If you think you are being overcharged, for example, or have been taken the 'scenic route', the advice is to pay the fare displayed on the taximeter, including extras, but make sure you get a receipt so that you can submit a copy of it with your complaint to the regulator.
- If a taxi driver refuses to carry you, let's say because he doesn't

want to bring you to your destination, you'll have to try to note the five-digit taxi licence number on the roof sign, or the car registration number.

- Beware of made-up 'extra' charges. Only specific extra charges are allowed: each additional adult; pick-up charge from a booking; premium rates at night-time and public holidays. Road tolls should be added to the fare and there should be no extra charge for airport pick-up or for luggage.

- If you lost something in a taxi and you booked your cab through an operator, contact them as soon as possible, as they should be able to help. If the driver can't return the item to you directly they may hand it in to a Garda station but most will try to return it to you directly if that is possible. The Gardaí are responsible for lost property handed in by taxi and hackney drivers and they will hang on to it for thirty-one days, so contact your local station.

- The regulator maintains a register of all wheelchair-accessible taxis and hackneys. If you have difficulty getting an accessible service, they may be able to provide you with contact details for an operator in your area.

- On the regulator's website there is an interactive tool that allows you to check the cost of the fare for a particular journey, by inputting the details of the journey and any extras.

- In addition the website includes a public register so you can input the five-digit licence number of the taxi or the vehicle licence registration number to check that the taxi or driver is properly licensed.

When a taxi driver can refuse to take you as a passenger:
- Where journeys are longer than thirty kilometres
- If passengers consume food or drink in the vehicle
- If passengers act in a disorderly, abusive or offensive manner
- If passengers are likely to soil or damage the vehicle

Who to Complain To

Rail travel

For information on your rights as a rail passenger and for un-resolved complaints contact the National Transport Authority's Public Transport Services Division: www.nationaltransport.ie/ 01-8798300.

Taxi complaints

For complaints relating to the conduct or behaviour of the taxi driver, the condition or cleanliness of the car, or overcharging you can complain to the Taxi Regulation Directorate: www. taxiregulation.nationaltransport.ie/076-1064000. You can also get in touch with the Gardaí if you notice any discrepancies with regard to licensing, tax or NCT requirements.

Legislation Name Check

Rail passenger rights

EC Regulation 1371/2007. Incorporated into Irish law as European Communities (Rail Passengers' Rights and Obligations) Regulations 2010. Statutory Instrument No 646 of 2010.

Taxis

Taxi Regulation Act 2003. No 25 of 2003.

Public Transport Regulation Act 2009.

14

Car Rental

Renting a car is commonplace for holidays abroad and has become increasingly common for trips at home too, given that owning and running a car has got so expensive. It should be a straightforward transaction; you see a price, pay it, pick up the requested car and off you go. In fact there are plenty of instances where things work out far from simply so this is a guide to knowing what to look out for and how to avoid the most common pitfalls.

In this Chapter
- Common problems
- Legislation
- Credit card rules
- Tips
- Who to complain to
- Legislation name check

Common Problems
If you know what the most persistent problems are, you'll know what to watch out for and consequently you'll be far less likely to encounter difficulties yourself. The problems listed below persist year on year and, according to consumer agencies, complaint levels are not falling.

Damage charges
Your credit card is charged for alleged damage, without your knowledge, after you return the car.

Advertised prices

What you see is not what you pay. 'Add-on' charges which are not optional are not clearly outlined, particularly with regard to fuel, insurance and location surcharge costs. These extras can greatly increase the final cost.

Breakdown/accident cover

For example, you are charged the 'excess' following an accident even when you are not at fault.

Fuel policy

Some consumers are charged in advance for a full tank of fuel and asked to return the car empty. No refunds are offered for unused fuel. This policy means that you'll inevitably pay more.

Car rental distribution websites

Inaccurate information is provided by car rental distribution websites about the terms and conditions of the partner car rental companies (age restrictions not explained, wrong opening hours, wrong type of vehicle or different cost of extras and insurance).

Insurance cover

The scope of the insurance policy may be unclear or additional insurance is automatically attached to the car rental contract and further charges are imposed on the consumer.

Insurance extras

Some of the car rental booking agents offer excess waiver insurance to consumers when they book their car and consumers are not aware that this insurance is provided by the booking agent and not by the car rental company. So when the consumer goes to collect their car, they are given the option of buying excess waiver insurance or leaving a deposit of the waiver amount with the company. In many cases the consumer will end up purchasing the car rental company's insurance even though they have already bought insurance, just to avoid having to leave a hefty deposit.

Legislation

There is no specific legislation covering car rental contracts. However, car rental contracts that are misleading or contain unfair terms would come under the Consumer Protection Act 2007 and the legislation on Unfair Terms in Consumer Contracts. This means that it's very important to read the terms and conditions so that you know what you are signing up for.

Credit Card Rules

Both Mastercard and Visa allow merchants to bill subsequent charges on the basis of a signed contract but their rules stipulate that they must advise the customer of the added charges before debiting. This applies to loss, theft or damage.

Beware: extra charges for petrol, parking fines and travel violations are permitted by Mastercard and Visa without further permission from the card-holder.

These rules mean that if the car rental company has debited your card for damage without telling you and you are disputing it, you can always contact your card-issuing bank about initiating a chargeback to get a refund if your complaint with the car rental company remains unresolved.

Tips
Before renting the car

- Are you booking directly from a car rental company or via an online agent? If the latter, then remember they are liable to return only the administration fee you paid them if something goes wrong. Your contract is with the car rental company so you'll have to complain to them.
- When looking for the best bargain, bear in mind that very often prices quoted online contain only the basics, so make sure you check what is included in the final quote and what is not.
- Always check the price of extras that you will need during

your rental: child seat, additional driver, extra insurance, collision damage waiver, excess.

- Pay special attention to the fuel policy; make sure it is explained to you clearly before you confirm the booking. 'Collect full return empty' policy implies that no refunds will be paid for unused fuel even if the whole tank was paid for up-front (often at a higher price than at the pumps). As it is impossible to return the car empty, especially during short rentals, an alternative policy should be available on request. A 'collect full return full' policy means that the vehicle should be provided with a full tank of fuel. Unless the consumer was clearly notified in the terms and conditions when booking the car, he should not have to prepay for fuel. It should be the consumer's responsibility to refuel the car with fuel of the correct type before it is returned. If the vehicle is not returned with a full tank, the consumer should bear the cost of refuelling.
- Check age restrictions.
- Make sure you are familiar with the cancellation policy.
- When renting abroad, familiarise yourself with the rules of the road.
- If you will be crossing a border make sure your insurance will cover you for the second country.

Collecting the car

- Make sure the car is what you ordered. If that is not available and they try to get you to pay extra, say no as you shouldn't have to pay more. If absolutely necessary, pay the extra but under duress, and complain in writing on your return.
- Make sure you understand what is covered by your insurance and what is not. It is also very important to know the excess amount that could be charged to your credit card in case of an accident. You can buy insurance to cover an excess waiver if you want.
- A staff member should check the condition of the car at the time of pick-up and mark all damages to the exterior and the

interior on a diagram. If you are not provided with a special check-list or diagram, make sure that you note any damages in writing and have your list signed by an employee of the car rental company.

- Always ask about the company policy in case of the car breaking down or in case of an accident.
- Make sure you know the type of fuel to use in your rental car.

During the rental

- If the car breaks down, phone the car rental company and follow the instructions provided. Do not get the vehicle repaired yourself without prior authorisation: if this is against the company's rules your money may not be refunded.
- In case of an accident, you should always note down the names and addresses of everyone involved. If anybody is injured, or if there is a dispute over who is responsible, you should notify the police. Contact the car rental company immediately.
- In the case of an accident or damage it is common practice for the excess to be charged to your card. However, this should be returned to you later if the accident or damage was not your fault.

Returning the car

- Try to return the car during the working hours of the car rental company and have it inspected by an employee. The condition of the vehicle should be confirmed in writing and signed both by the representative of the company and the driver.
- If you are returning the car outside the working hours of the car hire company, you should park it in the designated area. Take pictures of the vehicle as confirmation that it was returned in good condition.
- Remember to return with an empty or full tank depending on the terms (preferably full).
- If you booked your car rental through an agent you should

complain to them if, for example, the car provided doesn't match the one you booked or if there is no record of your having booked when you arrive at the rental office. But for any complaint relating to the rental itself, go to the rental company.

Who to Complain To

- If the company is abroad go to the European Consumer Centre for assistance: European Consumer Centre (ECC) Ireland/www.eccireland.ie/01-8797620.
- You can also go to the National Consumer Agency for information on your rights: www.consumerconnect.ie/1890-432432/01-4025555 or the Consumers' Association of Ireland: www.thecai.ie; 01-4978600.
- The Car Rental Council of Ireland runs a dispute service for complaints against its members: www.carrentalcouncil.ie/01-6761690.
- Don't forget the small claims procedure which can be used for claims against Irish or foreign companies. It costs €18 and you can claim up to €2000: www.courts.ie.
- If you have paid by Visa or Mastercard and the car rental company has broken its payment rules (see above), contact your credit-issuing bank, when other complaint avenues have failed, to see if you can initiate a chargeback.

Legislation Name Check

Misleading advertising, information and aggressive commercial practice
Directive 2005/29/EC on unfair business-to-consumer commercial practices in the internal market was transposed into Irish law by the Consumer Protection Act 2007 (No 19 of 2007).

Directive 2006/114/EC incorporated into Irish law by EC (misleading and comparative marketing communications) Regulations 2007. Statutory Instrument No 774 of 2007.

Unfair terms in consumer contracts

EC Directive 93/13/EEC: Incorporated into Irish law by EC (Unfair Terms in Consumer Contracts) Regulations. Statutory Instrument No 27 of 1995, as amended by the European Communities (Unfair Terms in Consumer Contracts) (Amendment) Regulations 2000, SI No 307 of 2000.

15

Accessing Healthcare Abroad

You know how to access healthcare in Ireland: you either pay the providers directly or through your private health insurance cover or use the public healthcare system or entitlements you have as a medical card holder. But what can you do if you are waiting too long for treatment or if a particular treatment isn't available in this country? Did you know that in some circumstances you are entitled to access healthcare abroad?

Then there are your pearly-whites to think of, especially as dental benefits for medical card holders and PRSI contributors have been severely reduced. Price comparison surveys show that dental services can be more expensive here so many opt to head to Northern Ireland or further afield. But what should you take into account before hopping on the train or heading for the airport?

In this Chapter
- How to access healthcare abroad
- Dental treatment abroad
- Focus: what pharmacists can do
- Who to complain to
- Legislation name check
- Accessing healthcare abroad

How to Access Healthcare Abroad
Under EU legislation you are entitled to seek healthcare in another Member State. Most EU citizens do not know they have this right: it

is barely used and quite complicated. However, new legislation is on the way which should simplify things. New provisions will do away with the need for prior authorisation for treatment abroad in some cases and will introduce national contact points for the provision of relevant information to patients.

In the meantime you are entitled to hospital care in the public healthcare system in another EU country to the same level as your entitlement here. However, you must have prior authorisation from your local Health Services Executive (HSE). Authorisation is granted on a case-by-case basis.

When you can seek authorisation

- If the treatment is not available in Ireland
- If there is urgent medical necessity
- If the treatment is a proven form of medical treatment
- If the treatment sought abroad is in a recognised hospital or other institution and under the control of a registered medical practitioner
- Where treatment cannot be provided in Ireland without undue delay

What do you have to do?

This scheme is run by the overseas department of the Health Services Executive and you must get a form E112 from your local HSE. The crucial thing is that a hospital consultant must give medical evidence with details of your condition and the type of treatment envisaged so you need the support of your doctor in order to apply.

The local HSE will decide to authorise or not but you are entitled to appeal. Once you are approved, the HSE is giving a commitment to pay the cost of the treatment and they should specify the nature and extent of treatment to be covered. Be aware that if the cost of treatment in the other country is higher than it is here, you will have to cover the difference yourself. The HSE may also agree to pay certain travel and subsistence costs for the patient and a travelling companion if the patient in question is a child or an elderly person.

Treatments that Irish residents have been approved for through the scheme include: plaque radiation therapy; deep brain stimulation surgery; bone-marrow transplant; cardiac transplant; stereotactic radiotherapy; lymphodema treatment; liver transplant; proton beam radiation; nasal potential difference testing.

The main countries that provide treatment to approved Irish residents are the United Kingdom, Sweden, Germany, France and Belgium.

Undue delay

Although this was not envisaged in the current legislation, cases taken to the European Court of Justice (ECJ) have resulted in 'undue delay' becoming a valid cause for seeking treatment abroad.

Cases taken in 1996 and 1998 clarified that patients who cannot access essential medical treatment within a reasonable timeframe in their own country have the right to access treatment in another Member State.

Another case taken to the ECJ in 2006 brought further clarification: that an institution may not refuse authorisation on the grounds of the existence of waiting lists as that 'distorts the normal order of priorities'. In other words, delay should depend on medical need rather then administrative timeframes and goals.

The National Treatment Purchase Fund

Established in 2002, the NTPF was an initiative under the government's health strategy to reduce long-term waiting lists, as at that time waiting lists were as long as two to five years.

Under the scheme, if you were a public patient waiting more than three months for in-patient procedures you could contact the NTPF and be referred for treatment. In the main you were sent to an Irish private hospital but the government paid for the treatment via its funding of the NTPF.

In 2011 it was announced that the NTPF was to be incorporated into a newly established Special Delivery Unit (SDU), with €20 million of the NTPF's €85million budget to be used to tackle hospital waiting lists. No further information on the changes was available at the time of writing so check with your doctor for updates.

The European Health Insurance Card

If you are travelling abroad in the EU for work or for holidays or if you are studying there, make sure you get your free European Health Insurance Card (EHIC). You will need one card for each family member. Apply to your local HSE or online at www.ehic. ie.

This card will give you access to the local public healthcare system of the country you are visiting, just as if you were a resident in that country.

On the www.ehic.ie website it's also worth checking the level of public healthcare that is provided in the country you are visiting. For example, in Spain some clinics have separate times for private and public patients, so make sure you're booking in as a public patient.

Dental Treatment Abroad

If you think dentists are too expensive here you are free to get your dental treatment elsewhere.

Many agencies have set up offices here to facilitate sending people to countries such as Hungary to get their teeth done. Having seen an increase in the numbers of patients from the Republic, many dentists in Northern Ireland cater for these patients by providing additional services like collection from train stations.

Whether you get your teeth done in Belfast, Budapest or Bray, you should always make sure that you are happy with your dentist. Ask about cost and procedures and whether the dentist is engaged in continuous training and ask about aftercare. No matter where you get your teeth seen to, problems could arise. But it's especially important if you are travelling to another country to make sure you do your research carefully.

- Ask your dentist what a procedure costs and then get a comparison from a dentist in the North or further afield.
- Take into account that different materials might be used, in crowns, fillings or dentures, and that this could affect the cost. Ask about this and about the difference in durability between materials used.
- Go to dentists who have been recommended to you, especially when travelling for treatment.
- Not all dentists in the North treat private patients from the Republic – some treat NHS patients solely. So ask around for recommendations.
- If travelling abroad, it is best to go to an agency that provides initial consultation with a dentist here.
- If you travelling abroad be aware that you may have to get a lot of work done in a limited timeframe, whereas if you were getting treatment at home it might be spread out and as a result be potentially less traumatic.
- Remember to take into account travel and accommodation

costs if travelling further afield.

- Make sure to ask about follow-up services: can they be carried out in Ireland or will you have to travel again?
- You could always mix and match by getting simple procedures such as cleaning, scraping and fillings from your local dentist and getting more extensive treatments done at keener prices in the North or abroad. Do check prices carefully, as travel costs may not make it worthwhile to travel far unless you need a lot of treatment carried out.
- Build a relationship with your dentist and never be shy to ask about the price of procedures. Under a new code of practice of dentists in Ireland prices for procedures should be displayed in dentists' surgeries. See Chapter 2.

If you are getting your dental work carried out in another EU country you are still entitled to tax relief at the standard rate on the payment made for non-routine treatments. Make sure to get the dentist to fill out the Med 2 form.

Your rights

Dental treatment is a service like any other, so you can expect it to be carried out with the necessary skill, due care and diligence and that any parts used should be of merchantable quality.

These rights apply across the EU and in Ireland you can also get in touch with the Dental Council if you want to report a member. If you are travelling abroad for treatment you might also want to check whether country codes of practice are in place for dentists.

Focus: What Pharmacists Can Do

It costs so much to go to the doctor that many people postpone and hope for the best. Another option is your local pharmacist. They can be your first port of call on your medical journey and consultation is free.

Since November 2010 pharmacies have been required to provide a dedicated consultation area so you can talk in private. The pharmacist might refer you to a doctor but you may have a condition that can be treated by over-the-counter medicine and thus avoid paying the doctor's fee.

What your pharmacist can help with:
- Provide the morning-after pill without prescription
- Help you perfect the right inhaler technique if you suffer from asthma
- Monitor your blood pressure and cholesterol
- Test your blood glucose
- Help with weight management and body mass index testing
- Baby-weighing services
- Flu vaccine

Specific ailments
- Skin rashes, runny noses, high temperatures
- Aches and pains, whether non-specific or a sports injury
- Sore throats, colds and headaches. Remember your GP may not prescribe an antibiotic so save yourself the trip
- Indigestion and stomach aches
- Personal issues such as constipation, haemorrhoids, bowel problems and your sexual health

When it comes to the cost of medicines, don't forget that generic brands may be available more cheaply than a well-known brand. However, if your doctor prescribes medicine and writes down a brand name on your prescription, your pharmacist is obliged to dispense exactly that and is not allowed to provide you with a cheaper generic version. When you visit the doctor, ask him or her to prescribe you a generic version to save yourself some money when you get to the pharmacy.

The Irish Pharmacy Union is campaigning to be allowed to provide more services in the frontline of healthcare. They would like to see the deregulation of some specific medicines so that they could provide them without prescriptions and if this were possible (as it is in many countries) you could save yourself the cost of a GP visit to pick up a prescription.

Legislation is also planned to enable pharmacists to substitute a cheaper generic drug for a branded drug on a prescription. Other proposals include pharmacists having the right to conduct clinical consultations with patients about taking medicine correctly and to dispense medication to medical-card holders without their having to get a prescription from their GP first.

Who to Complain To

If you have a problem always complain first to the service-provider. You can also turn to the National Consumer Agency (NCA) for information on your rights: www.consumerconnect.ie/1890-432432/01-4025555 and to the European Consumer Centre (ECC) Ireland: www.eccireland.ie/01-8797620 if you have a complaint against a dentist in another EU country.

For further healthcare information, enquiries and complaints
The Health Services Executive (HSE); www.hse.ie/1850-241850
European Health Insurance Card; ww.ehic.ie/1850-241850
The Irish Pharmaceutical Union; www.ipu.ie/01-4936401
The Dental Council of Ireland; www.dentalcouncil.ie/01-6762069
The Pharmaceutical Society of Ireland: www.thepsi.ie/01-2184000

Legislation Name Check

EC Regulation No 883/2004 of the European Parliament and of the Council on the coordination of social security systems.

16

Renting
and Management Companies

If you buy a property you will have to engage a solicitor to wade through the myriad deeds and contracts that need to be checked and signed. You will have to trust your solicitor and ask him/her to explain everything clearly to you so that you know what you're signing up for. But if you are renting accommodation there are plenty of clear rules that both you and your landlord must abide by. For example, you mightn't know that there are very specific timeframes laid down as to when you should give notice to leave or when the landlord can tell you to go.

If you own an apartment or a house in a development run by a management company there is new legislation that protects you so you need to know what these rules are.

In this Chapter
- Renting a home
- Your rental lease
- Management companies
- Who to complain to
- Legislation name check

Renting a Home
Although you don't own a rental property it is still your home. This means that you are entitled to your privacy and the landlord

is allowed to enter only with your pre-arranged permission. You can also have friends to stay but if somebody new is moving in you should tell the landlord.

Your home must comply with minimum standards. This means it should be free from damp, in good structural repair, have hot and cold water, adequate means of heating and ventilation, appliances in good working order, electrical wiring, gas and pipes in good repair and so on. The handy thing about renting is, of course, that the landlord and not you is obliged to carry our repairs, that is unless you have cause damage beyond normal wear and tear.

Bear in mind that it is up to you to pay any local authority charges, for example for bin collection, and if you've just moved in make sure you're not paying the arrears of previous tenants.

Your landlord's insurance policy is unlikely to cover your personal belongings so you might want to get your own contents insurance.

Remember your obligations: ask your landlord if there are any set conditions about parties and noise and whether you are allowed pets or can hang washing out on the balcony.

If you claim social welfare, are on a FÁS scheme or working part-time, you may qualify for help towards your rent and you may also get help with a deposit. If you are a full-time student or in a full-time job you are not normally eligible for rent supplement.

You are entitled to claim tax relief on rent. It is calculated at the lower tax band (20 per cent) and you can apply online on www.revenue.ie.

Your Rental Lease

All payments made to the landlord must be recorded either in the rent book or by written statement. The rent book or letting agreement (lease) must contain other information about the tenancy. Make sure to read everything carefully before you seal the deal and pay your deposit.

Information should include:

- Address of the rented dwelling
- Name and address of the landlord and his agent (if any)
- Name of the tenant
- Term of the tenancy
- Amount of rent and when and how it is to be paid, (e.g. cash, cheque, standing order)
- Details of other payments (e.g. telephone, television)
- Amount and purpose of any deposit paid and the conditions under which it will be returned to the tenant
- Statement of information on basic rights and duties of landlords and tenants
- Inventory of contents (and their condition)

Term of the lease

Most leases are for a fixed period of time, such as a year. If you are a student you'll have to be careful about signing a lease for a year if you need the accommodation for only nine months. If you can't find another person to rent it for the remaining three months of the lease and you break your lease, you will lose your deposit.

The landlord can terminate the tenancy without reason during the first six months but once the tenancy has lasted six months, the landlord will be able to end it only on specific grounds.

Acceptable grounds include the tenant not complying with their obligations (e.g. not paying their rent), the landlord intending to sell the dwelling and the landlord requiring the dwelling for his own occupation or for a family member.

The landlord must give you written notice of termination. The period of notice will depend on the duration of the tenancy, for example twenty-eight days within the first six months, fifty-six days after two years and eighty-four days after three years.

Deposits

Yes, you'll have to pay a deposit when you move in but you are entitled to get it back once you leave and it has to be returned promptly.

There are two situations, however, in which the landlord can keep the deposit or deduct some money from it. These are: 1) when there are rent arrears; and 2) where costs are incurred to repair damage above normal wear and tear.

Advertising or re-letting costs are not valid reasons for withholding a deposit and it is illegal for a landlord to hold a tenant's goods in lieu of money owed.

Rent arrears

If you are in arrears be aware that you are in breach of your tenancy obligations. The landlord will notify you in writing and if you have not met your rent arrears within fourteen days, he or she may issue you with twenty-eight days' notice of termination. You are entitled to formal notice of any claim that you have broken the tenancy conditions and to be given time to set things right.

Rent increases and reviews

Landlords can raise the rent only to the open market rate but it is difficult to prove what this might be. The landlord may raise the rent only once in a twelve-month period unless there has been a substantial change in the nature of the accommodation.

Given that rents have fallen over the past few years you may wish to ask your landlord for a rent review. Do your research on rent being paid for comparable properties in your area; take into account how long you've been there and the fact that you've been a good tenant and start negotiating.

Leaving your rented accommodation

It's likely that you'll be moving on at some point and you may as well do it correctly:

- Give notice in writing.
- Even if there is a verbal agreement with the landlord, put it in writing.
- Specify the current date and the day you plan to leave.
- The length of notice you have to give depends on how long you have been there: for example, less that six months, twenty-eight days; more than six months but less than a year, thirty-five days; one year but less than two years, forty-two days; more than two years, fifty-six days.
- You can give twenty-eight days notice any time if the landlord is in breach of his obligations but do give the landlord a chance to fix things first.

Management Companies

Do you live in a development but have no idea what your main-tenance fee covers? Maybe the grass isn't being cut and the place isn't kept in repair; maybe your fee is going up and you feel you don't have a say. Have you ever attended the annual general meeting of the company and voted on something that affects your home? As an owner you are, in fact, a member of the management company and as such, have voting rights.

New legislation governing management companies came into force in 2011, which gives you some protection where there was little or nothing before. It covers developments where there are at least five residential units with shared amenities, facilities and services.

What is a management company?

If you are the owner of an apartment or house in an apartment complex or a gated estate, it will have several common areas acces-sible to all the residents. These typically include the lobbies, stairwells, lifts, main corridors and entrance gates.

There may be other areas that the owners share, such as the roofing, and possibly some common parking places and gardens around the development.

New housing schemes and apartment blocks have a management company, which is responsible for the maintenance of these shared spaces and services. This is because typically when you buy in a development you buy a leasehold. This means that you own the home but not the land it's built on. The management company owns the freehold of the common areas of the development on behalf of the owners and the owners share collective responsibility for them.

Management companies can be an efficient means of management as they offer structure for administration and ownership. A management company is compulsory in a multi-unit development.

The rules
The Multi-Units Developments Act 2011 addresses a number of areas:

- The developer must establish an owners' management company at his expense.
- The developer must transfer common areas to the legal ownership of the owners' management company before any units have sold. In the case of existing developments ownership must be transferred within six months of the commencement of the Act (i.e. by 1 October 2011).
- If there is no sinking fund in place (a fund established for 'rainy day' or big shared expenses) one must be set up by 1 October 2012.
- The sinking fund should be set up with a payment of €200 per annum or another amount as agreed by members.
- With regard to voting rights the general rule is that there should be one vote per residential unit. In mixed-use developments other voting arrangements can be put in place as long as they are fair and equitable.

- Annual meetings must be held and annual reports prepared for members.
- Service charges and other expenditure must be approved by members at a general meeting.
- A dispute resolution mechanism will be available (via a new circuit court jurisdiction) to deal with disputes between parties. The court can require parties to engage in a mediation process.

In some complexes, developers have retained voting rights and even given themselves preferential votes, meaning they have an overall majority at an AGM. This may mean that you and other owners have been locked out of the voting process and haven't been able to make decisions about how the company is run, whether an agent is hired, changing the service-provider, who maintains the grounds and so on. Unless a developer has circuit court approval they cannot do this from now on. With one vote per residential unit, you and the other owners have an equal say in how your development is organised and run. You can set the budget and hire and fire contractors, including the agent if there is one.

Who to Complain To

The Private Residential Tenancies Board (PRTB)
For disputes relating to a private tenancy agreement go to the PRTB. You can also submit a complaint to them if you find a landlord in breach of his or her legal obligations: www.prtb.ie/01-6350600.

Threshold
For information on your rights as a tenant: www.threshold.ie.

Legislation Name Check

The Residential Tenancies Act 2004. Act No 27 of 2004.

The Multi-Unit Developments Act 2011. Act No 2 of 2011.

17

How to Complain

If a service has not been provided adequately or if a product is faulty and you know you are legally entitled to a remedy, what's so bad about asking for it? Consumer legislation is there to redress the balance of power between the consumer and the business – so use it. It doesn't have to be emotional and it's not a confrontation. Instead it is you being calm and informed and asking for what you deserve. You have entered into a contract with the retailer or service-provider and if something goes wrong the negotiation should continue in the same professional manner.

Remember it's a two-way process as the consumer and the business need each other. From a business perspective looking after an existing customer is easier and cheaper than finding a new one. Empowered consumers who know their rights and complain when necessary are good for business as they are likely to shop more and tell others about their positive experiences. Consumers with negative experiences will pass on the negative. Businesses need to realise this and ensure their staff are adequately trained and that a decent complaints procedure is in place. There will always be complaints but it's how a business handles them that matters.

In this Chapter
- Complaining effectively
- Making the complaint
- Writing the letter
- Sample Letters (Product, Service, Airline)

Complaining Effectively

There are four keys to this: acting quickly; knowing your rights; knowing what you want; and remaining focused and polite.

Act quickly

Act promptly when something goes wrong; otherwise you run the risk of being deemed to have accepted a faulty product.

Under EU consumer law, during the first six months your rights are highest as you don't have to prove the defect. Under Irish law you have six years in which to make a claim but don't let that make you complacent. Your rights are always strongest close to the time of purchase and you also have to take into account the expected life span of the product and inevitable wear and tear.

Under some consumer laws there are time limits. For example you must write your letter of complaint about a package holiday within twenty-eight days, or about damaged luggage within seven days and delayed luggage within twenty-one days. If you've bought something online your cooling-off period, the time when you can change your mind, is a minimum of seven days.

Know your rights

To complain effectively you need to know if you have grounds for a complaint. Find out what your rights are so that you are sure the retailer or service-provider is obliged to provide a remedy. For example, a shop is not obliged to take back a perfect but unwanted item, (unless purchased from a distance or at the doorstep where you have your cooling-off period). Or if you break something yourself you are not entitled to a remedy. So if you know that and are asking for goodwill, you'll need to ask for it in an appropriate way.

Knowing your rights are also gives you a certain amount of power. It will ensure that you can confidently stand your ground and not let someone fob you off, telling you that they owe you nothing.

Know what you want
Once you know what your entitlements are, you will be able to decide what you want.

For example, are you looking for repair, replacement or refund or for compensation for damaged luggage? Being clearer will help: if the retailer or service-provider comes back to you with a suggested remedy you need to know if you are happy to accept it or wish to negotiate further.

Remain focused and polite
Be firm but polite. Never get aggressive, no matter what the situation is. If you know your entitlements you can negotiate with the company on strong terms. Always focus on the positive action you want them to take rather than your disappointment. If you allow yourself to get emotional you will be less clear-headed.

Do be determined. If you know you are right, don't back down. Many people do back down and in certain cases you will have to be relentless and persevere. You will get there.

Making the Complaint
Stage 1
The first thing to do is to go back to where you bought the product or service. Depending on the circumstances, it may be best to make your complaint first either face to face or over the phone. If it is a small(ish) business for example, you should be able to speak to the manager to address your complaint directly to him or her. If it's a bigger company, check if it has an internal complaints procedure or a customer service department that deals with complaints and address your complaint to it.

If you telephone a service-provider about a complaint you are often talking to a different person each time. Keep records of the calls and names but if this happens you'll need to put the complaint in writing to the customer service section.

When it comes to complaining about faulty electrical items, the retailer will often refer you to the manufacturer. This is fine if you have a valid warranty but bear in mind that with or without a manufacturer's warranty it is the retailer who has the legal obligation to remedy.

Always give the business the opportunity to put things right: the majority of complaints should be resolved at this stage.

Stage 2

If making a verbal complaint hasn't worked, it's time to put it in writing. Be clear and concise in your letter. Don't give unnecessary detail or be rude about the retailer or explain your feelings. To be blunt about it, no one needs your life story. You just need to explain what happened and when, and what you want to happen now. Include references to people you have already spoken to in the company, copies of any previous correspondence and a copy of your receipt, credit card statement or order confirmation as proof of purchase.

There is generally little point in copying your letter to the MD, TDs and the Taoiseach. A letter to the appropriate person should be fine.

What next?

If none of this has worked there are other places you can turn to for help for your unresolved complaint, depending on the area of complaint. Check out public bodies, industry bodies or professional associations.

At the end of each section in this book you will find contact details of the relevant complaints bodies. There is also a section on the small claims procedure which might be your next option and a list of alternative dispute resolution bodies and other organisations is contained in the Who's Who section.

Writing the Letter

In your letter you should be concise and to the point and ask clearly for what you want.

- Write to the manager by name if you can or else to the customer service department.
- If you were talking to a salesperson give their name.
- Be factual and get straight to the point; don't add unnecessary detail.
- Do not use emotive terms or condemnation such as 'You are all idiots' or 'I am distraught.' You can tell the company you are disappointed in the product or service delivery but too much emotion won't help matters.
- If sending by post, register the letter so that you have proof or postage and don't forget to keep a copy. If sending by email, you'll have a copy but don't delete it.

Letter format

- Start with when and where you bought the item and how much you paid. Mention that you are attaching proof of purchase.
- Describe what happened: for example, the television broke down or you were overcharged in the final bill.
- State what you did next: for example, you telephoned the manager or spoke to customer service, and describe the outcome.
- State what you want to happen next: for example, a refund or replacement. Add that you are aware you are entitled to this and name the relevant consumer legislation.
- End by suggesting a timeframe for them to respond to you: for example, ten days. You could also mention that if the complaint is unresolved you will take further action, such as a small claim, arbitration or pursuing relevant complaints procedure if there is one.
- Copy any proof of purchase or other relevant documentation such as photographs or expert opinion.

Sample Letter 1: Faulty Product

Mary Manager
Shop
Main Street
Nicetown
Date

Dear Ms Manager

I bought [give a precise description of what you bought, including colour, model and price and stating when you bought it] in your shop in Nicetown.

I enclose evidence of purchase: [for example, a receipt or credit card statement and enclose a copy (not the original). You could also enclose a copy of a description or advertisement if that is relevant].

When I tried to use this item/I discovered that [say what went wrong and what the product did not do, if it was not 'as described' etc.].

I went back to your shop and the shop assistant, Seamus Pleasant, said that complaints were dealt with by your department *or* Further to our telephone conversation on [date] I would like to put my complaint in writing to you.

I would like you to [tell them exactly what you want: for example, repair, replacement, or refund].

I believe I am entitled to this under consumer law. [Name the legislation to show you know what you are talking about. This will make the letter stronger, especially if this is your second complaint or if talking to the manager has got you nowhere.]

I look forward to your reply within ten days and hope this matter can be sorted out quickly. If I do not hear from you I will take my complaint to the [name the relevant complaints body: for example, small claims procedure/ ombudsman].

Yours sincerely
Annie Irish

Sample Letter 2: Service

[Address]

[Date]

Dear Ms Manager

On [date] you carried out/I subscribed to [describe service] at a cost of [name price paid].

I enclose evidence of purchase: [for example, a receipt or credit card statement and a copy (not the original). You could also enclose order information or a copy of a description or advertisement if that is relevant].

This service was [say what went wrong: for example, the service was not carried out with skill or parts used were faulty, or you are not receiving a service subscription that you paid for].

I would like you to [tell them exactly what you want: for example, repair, replacement, or refund].

I believe I am entitled to this under consumer law. [Name the legislation to show you know what you are talking about. This will make the letter stronger, especially if this is your second complaint or if talking to the manager has got you nowhere.]

I look forward to your reply within ten days and hope this matter can be sorted out quickly. If I do not hear from you I will proceed to take my complaint to the [name the relevant complaints body: for example, small claims procedure/ombudsman].

Yours sincerely

Joe Punter

Sample Letter 3: To an Airline

Customer Service
[Address]
[Date]

Dear Sir/Madam

I am writing to you regarding [insert problem: for example, lost/damaged/delayed luggage/cancelled flight/delayed flight].

I was on/due to fly on [give flight number and departure and destination airport and date of travel].

Unfortunately, [explain what happened: for example, the flight was cancelled/delayed, your luggage was damaged, delayed or lost].

I would like [explain what you are looking for. Find out what you are entitled to first: for example, compensation for lost luggage or a reimbursement for a cancelled flight].

I belive I am enitled to this under consumer law [name legislation].

I look forward to hearing from you within ten days and I hope this matter can be resolved. If I do not hear from you I will proceed to take my complaint to the [name the relevant complaints body: for example, Commission for Aviation Regulation].

Yours sincerely

Janet Flyer

18

The Small Claims Procedure

Let's say that your washing machine has broken down or a plumber ruined your carpet while carrying out repairs in your home. You know you have rights and you ask for them. But the retailer or service-provider refuses. So you write a letter of complaint but maybe that doesn't resolve anything either.

Your next step may be to take small claims action.

In this Chapter
- The small claims procedure
- Who can I claim against?
- How to apply
- How the procedure works
- After court
- Useful websites
- Legislation name check

The Small Claims Procedure
The procedure provides cheap and easy access to justice for consumer complaints. You pay a non-refundable fee of €18 and you can claim up to €2000. The procedure is run through the district court system.

The court hearing small claims does not sit permanently but only on certain days. Some courts may have the flexibility to add more sittings to cater for the demand. For example, the Dublin city centre small claims procedure sits once a month, while in many towns small claims court sits once every two months or even less often. You might have twenty to thirty claims at a sitting. This means that even if you apply today you will have to wait as your case might not get into the next court's sitting.

Types of claim

The small claims procedure does not cover debt claims, personal injury or rental issues; it is for issues relating to products or services.

The most common types of claims submitted relate to holidays, cars and electrical goods, followed by furniture, damage to property, dry-cleaners, building and professional services.

Who Can I Claim Against?

You can claim against a business or company but not against an individual. However some registrars seem to apply some flexibility here as I have heard from people who have successfully taken claims against tradespeople who were not registered as businesses but were carrying out work in the course of their business.

Since 1 January 2009 it has been possible to submit a small claim against any business or company in the EU by means of the European Small Claims Procedure. It works in the same way as the regular procedure, except that you cannot submit your complaint online.

Since the beginning of 2010, small businesses (SMEs) can use the small claims procedure to claim against another business and can also use the European small claims procedure. The threshold and application procedure remain the same.

How to Apply

Fortunately the application system is pretty simple. There is a one-page form where you include both your address (you're the claimant) and the name and address of the business/company you're claiming against (the respondent) and then a paragraph explaining the problem and detailing how much you are claiming for.

You should add any evidence that may be relevant. This may include:

- A copy of any complaint letter/s sent and response/s received
- Photos, if relevant
- Expert statements if relevant (i.e. from a mechanic or electrician or dentist)
- A copy of proof of purchase: for example, receipt/credit card statement
- The €18 non-refundable fee

This can all be done online at www.courts.ie. You will be prompted for the relevant information so this is probably the easiest way to apply and in fact the majority of applications are now submitted this way.

Key things to know when applying
- You send the claim to the district court nearest the respondent's address and not the one nearest to you.
- You must have the respondent's legal business or company name and not their trading name, which may be different. You can find this out at the Companies Registration Office at www.cro.ie. There you can do a free search or pay €3.50 to get more detailed information if you need it.

How the Procedure Works
You submit your claim and the small claims registrar will assess it and may have to contact you for further information. Then they will contact the respondent who has at least fifteen days to respond (some courts will give longer).

Then one of three things can happen:

1. *Your claim is not disputed*

If the respondent admits your claim he/she is required to notify the registrar's office by returning a Notice of Acceptance of Liability form. The district court will then make an order in your favour (without your having to attend court) for the amount claimed and direct that it be paid within a short specific period of time. A majority of eligible claims are settled this way.

2. *The respondent doesn't reply*

If the respondent does not reply to the initial correspondence from the Small Claims Registrar within the timeframe, you (the claimant) win by default, as the claim is treated as undisputed.

3. *Your claim is disputed*

If the Small Claims Registrar receives a notice from the respondent disputing your claim or making a counterclaim against you, the registrar will contact you and let you have a copy of the respondent's answer. If this happens the registrar may interview and negotiate with both parties to try to reach an agreement if this happens.

A date in court

If your complaint hasn't been resolved at the initial stage it will be listed for a court hearing. Your claim may not be listed immediately if the office is still waiting for correspondence from the respondent. This is why it's a good idea that you, the claimant, keep in contact with the small claims office to make sure your case is followed up on and given a court date.

Let's say the respondent made a counterclaim, you submitted more information and the respondent did not reply to that. The small claims office will list your case as open and won't act because they are still waiting for a response. Months can pass and this case should be listed for court but the technical resources are not in place to ensure that his happens. So you should contact the office and ask for your case to be checked. If time has passed and there has been no new correspondence from the respondent, you should ask for your case to be listed for court. In some instances you will be asked to put this in writing.

If you've applied online you can check online for updates to your file, using the reference number you were given. If there are none, contact the office and request a court hearing.

When the day comes there will be plenty of other claims being heard and some judges, once they have roll-called everyone, will ask the claimants and respondents to step outside and try and resolve their differences amicably. Those who can't find a resolution will go back into the courtroom and the judge will give his or her ruling.

It will take only a matter of minutes, there will be plenty of people around and it is not a scary courtroom set-up like you see in the movies! There is no need for a solicitor. Some companies will send legal representation in on their behalf but this won't have any effect on your case. You should bring all your documentation and you can bring a witness if you feel you need to.

Note that if you do end up in court you will have to pay for your own travel and expenses and the cost of taking time off work.

After Court
Typically around a quarter of claims end up scheduled for a court date. But some will be settled or withdrawn before the date arrives. Some cases that end up in court will be dismissed by the judge but many other consumers will win their cases.

Once a court order is issued to the business or company you will be notified and the respondent has approximately four weeks to pay up. If they don't pay up you can ask for the sheriff to execute the court order (decree). Admittedly, in a minority of cases, this doesn't work. Either party can appeal to the circuit court if they are unhappy with the judge's decision. This will involve legal costs although the circuit court could award you costs if you win.

Useful Website

www.courts.ie

Legislation Name Check

District Court Rules 1997: Statutory Instrument No 93 of 1997.

Regulation (EC) No 861/2007 establishing a European Small Claims Procedure: District Court (European Small Claims) Rules 2008. SI No 583 of 2008.

District Court (Small Claims) Rules 2009, Statutory Instrument No 519 of 2009. (Small business-to-business claims).

19

Who's Who

When it comes to consumer rights and who is in charge of what, there are so many different official bodies that it's a bit of minefield. So this section brings them all together as a sort of reference guide.

Many of the bodies listed here also give information and run complaints procedures. These are also listed in each section of this book according to the topic being discussed.

In this Chapter
- Government departments responsible for consumer policy
- Public agencies
- National consumer organisations
- Consumer education
- Redress: Court and Alternative Dispute Resolution (ADR)

Government Departments Responsible for Consumer Policy

Department of Enterprise, Trade and Employment (DETE)
This department is responsible for consumer policy: its development and the enforcement of a regulatory framework.
Contact details
Competition and Consumer Policy Section, Earlsfort Centre, Dublin 2; www.entemp.ie/01-6312121

Department of Health and Children
This department is responsible for food safety and labelling, as well

as the safety of medicinal products.
Contact details
Hawkins House, Hawkins Street, Dublin 2;
www.dohc.ie/01-6354000

Department of Finance
This department is responsible for policy relating to consumer credit.
Contact details
Government Buildings, Upper Merrion St, Dublin 2;
www.finance.gov.ie/01-6767571

Department of Communications, Energy and Natural Resources
This department is responsible for the policy on communications, broadcasting and energy.
Contact details
29-31 Adelaide Road, Dublin 2; www.dcenr.ie/01-6782000

Department of Transport
This department is responsible for policy on aviation and public transport.
Contact details
Transport House, 44 Kildare St, Dublin 2;
www.transport.ie/01-6707444

Department of Justice, Equality and Law Reform
This department is responsible for providing the courts service.
Contact details
94 St. Stephen's Green, Dublin 2; www.justice.ie/01-6028292

Public Agencies
National Consumer Agency (NCA)
The NCA is the statutory body charged with representing the voice of consumers and enforcing consumer legislation. It also conducts targeted research and education and awareness activities and is responsible for market surveillance in respect of product safety. In

addition the NCA provides information to consumers on financial products and services and carries out price-comparison surveys relating to financial products. The NCA runs an information and advice line for consumers.

Contact details

4 Harcourt Road, Dublin 2; www.consumerconnect.ie/www. itsyourmoney.ie/www.consumerproperty.ie; 1890-432432/01-4025555

Commission for Aviation Regulation (CAR)

An independent public body under the auspices of the Department of Transport, the commission regulates certain aspects of the aviation travel and trade sectors in Ireland. From a consumer point of view CAR enforces the legislation governing air passenger right and passengers with reduced mobility and have a complaints process for passengers.

Contact details

3rd Floor Alexandra House, Earlsfort Terrace, Dublin 2; www.aviationreg.ie/01-6611700

Commission for Communications Regulation (ComReg)

ComReg is the statutory body responsible for the regulation of the electronic communications sector (telecommunications, radio communications and broadcasting transmission) and the postal sector. Since 2010 it has also regulated the premium rate service industry, taking over that role from REGTEL. It runs a complaints process for consumers in relation to communication services and premium rate services.

Contact details

Block DEF, Abbey Court, Irish Life Centre, Lower Abbey Street, Dublin 1; www.askcomreg.ie/www.callcosts.ie/ www.phonesmart.ie/1890-229668/01-8049668

Commission for Energy Regulation (CER)

The commission promotes competition in the electricity and natural gas sectors and protects the interests of consumers. CER licenses electricity and natural gas companies and sets performance standards, which it also enforces. The CER has an energy customers' team that provides an independent complaints resolution service for customers who have unresolved complaints with their supplier or network operator.

Contact details
The Exchange, Belgard Square North, Tallaght, Dublin 24;
www.cer.ie/www.energycustomers.ie/1890-404404

Competition Authority

The Competition Authority is an independent statutory body responsible for enforcing Irish and European competition law. It takes action against anti-competitive practices, such as price-fixing, and blocks anti-competitive business mergers. The authority also has a role in informing government, public authorities, businesses and the wider public about competition issues.

Contact details
14 Parnell Square, Dublin 1;
www.tca.ie/01-8045400/1890-220224

Food Safety Authority of Ireland (FSAI)

The principal function of the FSAI is to take all reasonable steps to ensure that food produced, distributed or marketed in the state meets the highest standards of food safety and hygiene and to ensure that food complies with legal requirements, or with recognised codes of good practice. Consumers can contact the FSAI with complaints regarding unsafe practices in premises serving or selling food.

Contact details
Abbey Court, Lower Abbey Street, Dublin 1;
www.fsai.ie/1890-336677/01-8171300

Safefood

An all-Ireland body, responsible for the promotion of food safety on the island of Ireland. It was established in 1999 under the terms of the British-Irish Agreement Act 1999 and the North-South Cooperation (Implementation Bodies) Northern Ireland Order

1999. The organisation is responsible for the: promotion of food safety; research into food safety; communication of food alerts; surveillance of food-borne disease; promotion of scientific co-operation and laboratory linkages and the development of cost-effective facilities for specialised laboratory testing.

Contact details
Cork: 7 Eastgate Avenue, Eastgate, Little Island, County Cork
Dublin: Block B, Abbey Court, Lower Abbey Street, Dublin 1
www.safefood.eu/1850-404567/Cork: 021-2304100/
Dublin: 01-4480600

National Transport Authority (NTA)

Established in 2009, the National Transport Authority (NTA) is responsible for securing the provision of public passenger land transport services: for example, bus and rail. Since January 2011 the NTA has also assumed responsibility for the regulation of taxis, hackneys and limousines. The staff of the former Commission for Taxi Regulation were incorporated into the NTA as the Taxi Regulation Directorate at that time. The directorate accepts complaints in relation to taxi services. In addition the NTA accepts complaints about rail passenger services.

Contact details
Taxi complaints: 35 Fitzwilliam Square, Dublin 2;
www.taxiregulation.nationaltransport.ie/076-1064000
Rail passenger complaints: Dún Scéine, Iveagh Court,
Harcourt Lane, Dublin 2; www.nationaltransport.ie/01-8798300

Broadcasting Authority of Ireland (BAI)

Established in 2009, the BAI's role is to ensure that our broadcasting services best serve our needs, that democratic values, such as freedom of expression, are upheld and that our broadcasting service is open and pluralistic. The BAI incorporates work previously undertaken by the Broadcasting Commission of Ireland and the Broadcasting Complaints Commission and accepts consumer complaints.

Contact details
2-5 Warrington Place, Dublin 2; www.bai.ie/01-6441200

Irish Medicines Board (IMB)
The Irish Medicines Board (IMB) protects and enhances human and animal health through the regulation of human and veterinary medical products. The IMB regulates clinical trials and monitors and inspects products on the market to ensure their safety and efficacy. Enforcement activities include investigation of potential breaches of regulations and a range of measures, including prosecution, may be applied.
Contact details
Kevin O'Malley House, Earlsfort Centre, Earlsfort Terrace, Dublin 2; www.imb.ie/01-6764971

Irish Dental Council
The Irish Dental Council was established under the provisions of the Dentists Act 1985. It maintains and publishes a register of dentists and a register of dental specialists. The council promotes high standards in professional education and professional conduct among dentists. It also has the power to conduct enquiries in the fitness of a registered dentist to practice dentistry on grounds of, among other things, alleged professional misconduct.
Contact details
57 Merrion Square, Dublin 2; www.dentalcouncil.ie/01-6762069

The Pharmaceutical Society of Ireland (PSI)
The PSI is an independent statutory body established by the Pharmacy Act 2007. It protects the health and safety of consumers by regulating pharmacy services. In addition to registering pharmacists and pharmacies, the PSI's role includes accreditation of educational programmes, inspection and enforcement and receiving and acting on complaints received about pharmacists and pharmacy owners.

Contact details
18 Shrewsbury Road, Ballsbridge, Dublin 4;
www.thepsi.ie/01-2184000

The Opticians Board

Established under the provisions on the Opticians Act 1956 and 2003, the Opticians Board maintains a register of optometrists and dispensing opticians. The board is funded wholly by registration and retention fees paid by registered members. Complaints alleging breaches of the Opticians Act or of board rules may be investigated by the board.
Contact details
18 Fitzwilliam Square, Dublin 2;
www.opticiansboard.ie/01-6767416

National Standards Authority of Ireland (NSAI)

The NSAI operates under the National Standards Authority of Ireland Act 1985 and is Ireland's official standards body. It is the certification authority for CE marking and further protects consumers by issuing certification that goods conform to applicable safety and quality standards. In addition the authority assesses and approves new materials and processes for the construction industry and has an information provision role. The Legal Metrology Service is part of the NSAI and regulates and supervises weights and measures (for example airport weighing scales, food weighing scales in supermarkets and measures for alcoholic drinks).
Contact details
(Headquarters) 1 Swift Square, Northwood, Santry, Dublin 9;
www.nsai.ie/01-8073800

Citizens' Information Board

A statutory body that provides information, advice and advocacy on a range of social and public services. Information and advice include consumer issues. It supports the nationwide voluntary network of Citizens' Information Centres and funds and supports the Money Advice and Budgeting Service (MABS).

Contact details
www.citizensinformation.ie/1890-777121/your local CIC;
www.mabs.ie/1890-83438/your local MABS office

National Consumer Organisations
Consumers' Association of Ireland (CAI)
The Consumers' Association of Ireland is an independent, non-profit organisation established in 1966. The aim of the CAI is independently to protect, promote and represent the interests of consumers. The CAI is a registered charity and membership is open to all who wish to pay an annual subscription. The CAI publishes a monthly magazine called *Consumer Choice,* which contains reports on various products and on consumer issues and presents case studies illustrating consumer rights. Volunteers run a free consumer advice line which is open to all.
Contact details
43-44 Chelmsford Road, Ranelagh, Dublin 6;
www.thecai.ie/01-4978600

European Consumer Centre (ECC) Ireland
ECC Ireland is part of the European Consumer Centre Network that exists in twenty-nine European countries and is funded jointly and equally by the European Commission and the Irish government via the National Consumer Agency. It offers consumers advice on rights when shopping in another European state. The ECC Ireland also offers a dispute-resolution service and if necessary can liaise directly with a trader via its sister centre in the country of purchase. In addition ECC Ireland offers advice on and access to dispute resolution mechanisms such as mediation and arbitration for unresolved complaints relating to cross-border services.
Contact details
MACRO Centre, 1 Green Street, Dublin 7;
www.eccireland.ie/01-8797647

Consumer Education
Dolceta
An online consumer education project financed by the European Commission, involving twenty-seven countries of the EU. Each country has its own site and Dolceta Ireland offers detailed information on consumer rights and consumer finance. In addition the site included online modules for teachers, which focus on different consumer topics.

Contact details
www.dolceta.eu/ireland

Alternative Dispute Resolution (ADR)

An ADR body is an organisation that aims to resolve disputes without going to court. There are two main types of ADR: arbitration and mediation.

Arbitration is a consensual procedure for the settlement of disputes. The parties agree to be bound by the decision of the arbitrator, which is final and legally binding on both parties. In Ireland arbitration is governed by the Arbitration Acts 1954-98.

With mediation, as in arbitration, the parties agree to use a neutral third party to help to resolve a dispute. However the terms of the agreement are decided by the parties rather than by the mediator. This is not legally binding or enforceable through the courts but an agreement made in this way can be put into a legally binding format.

Arbitration and mediation both offer a useful alternative to court: they are generally less costly, less time-consuming and can often be completed at a distance.

There are other forms of ADR but when it comes to consumer disputes these are the methods typically used.

Redress, Court and Alternative Dispute Resolution (ADR)

Small Claims Procedure: see *Chapter 19*

European Small Claims Procedure: see *Chapter 19*

Nominated ADR Bodies in Ireland

In order to provide access to justice by non-court methods for European consumers, the European Commission has developed a recommendation on the provision of arbitration (Recommendation 98/257/EC) and another on the provision of mediation (Recommendation 2001/310/EC). When bodies comply with these recommendations it means that minimum-quality guarantees are in place.

For this reason the Department of Enterprise, Trade and Employment (DETE) has nominated the Irish ADR bodies listed below as adhering to one or other of the recommendations. The bodies are then included in a database published on the European Commission website.

In Ireland DETE liaises with the European Consumer Centre (ECC) with regard to nominating ADR bodies and the ECC can advise and assist consumers in accessing ADR procedures for the resolution of cross-border complaints. The list below includes bodies that provide out-of-court dispute resolution mechanisms for consumers but are not nominated by DETE as complying with Commission recommendations.

These bodies are also very useful resources for consumers: one reason why they may not comply with the recommendations is that they may not be wholly independent, perhaps receiving some funding from the industry they represent.

Advertising Standards Authority of Ireland (ASAI)

The Advertising Standards Authority for Ireland is an independent regulatory body set up to ensure that all advertisements shown in Ireland are legal, decent, honest and truthful. It is financed by the advertising industry and is committed to promoting the highest standards of marketing communications in advertising, promotional marketing and direct marketing. The ASAI also deals with individual complaints.

Contact details

IPC House, 35-39 Shelbourne Road, Dublin 4; www.asai.ie/01-6608766

The Financial Services Ombudsman's Bureau

The Financial Services Ombudsman is a statutory officer who deals independently with complaints from consumers about their individual dealings with any of the financial service-providers. To submit your complaint to this service you must first have tried to resolve it with the company. In addition to individual consumers, limited companies with a turnover of €3m or less, unincorporated bodies, charities, clubs, partnerships and trusts can use the service. The bureau can award compensation of up to €250,000 and decisions are binding subject to appeal to the High Court.

Contact details

3rd Floor, Lincoln House, Lincoln Place, Dublin 2; www.financialombudsman.ie/1890-882090/01-6620899

The Office of the Pensions Ombudsman

The Pensions Ombudsman investigates and gives decisions on complaints and disputes involving occupational pension schemes and personal retirement savings accounts (PRSAs).

Contact details

36 Upper Mount Street, Dublin 2; www.pensionsombudsman.ie/01-6471650

Scheme for Tour Operators, Chartered Institute of Arbitrators

The Chartered Institute of Arbitrators (Irish branch) is the authority for the regulation, administration, training and promotion of arbitration in Ireland. They have some six hundred members in the Irish branch and this scheme arbitrates on disputes relating to

package holidays.
Contact details
Merchant's House, 27-30 Merchant's Quay, Dublin 8;
www.arbitration.ie/01-7079739

Other Out-of-Court Bodies Involved in the Resolution of Consumer Disputes
The Direct Selling Association of Ireland
This has been the recognised trade association for the direct selling industry since 1981. Their consumer code of practice is designed to champion fair selling methods and offer legal rights to consumers that exceed those required by law.
Contact details
Avalon, Ballytrust, Ballinagh, County Cavan;
www.dsai.ie/049-4367765

The Private Residential Tenancies Board (PRTB)
The PRTB was established in September 2004 to resolve disputes between landlords and tenants. It also operates a national tenancy registration system and provides information and policy advice on the private rented sector. The PRTB dispute-resolution service replaces the courts in relation to the majority of landlord and tenant disputes.
Contact details
2nd Floor, O'Connell Bridge House, d'Olier Street, Dublin 2;
www.prtb.ie/01-6350600

The Personal Injuries Assessment Board (PIAB)
The PIAB, now known as InjuriesBoard.ie is a statutory body, which provides independent assessment of personal injury compensation for victims of workplace, motor and public liability accidents. The funding of InjuriesBoard.ie operations is met primarily by levying fees on respondents.
Contact details
PO BOX 8, Clonakilty, County Cork;
www.injuriesboard.ie/1890-829121

The Society of the Irish Motor Industry (SIMI)

SIMI is the official voice of the motor industry in Ireland. It is a members' organisation, consisting of dealers, repairers, vehicle distributors, wholesalers, retailers, vehicle testers and other operators within the industry in Ireland. The SIMI Standards Tribunal can be contacted to resolve consumers' disputes.

Contact details

5 Upper Pembroke Street, Dublin 2; www.simi.ie/01-6761690

The Car Rental Council of Ireland

The representative trade organisation for the car rental industry in Ireland. Membership of the council is open to companies operating a year-round car rental business with a minimum fleet size of thirty vehicles and is subject to acceptance of and compliance with the council's constitution and code of practice. The council operates a dispute-resolution service for consumers.

Contact details

5 Upper Pembroke St, Dublin 2;
www.carrentalcouncil.ie/01-6761690

Mediation Forum Ireland (MFI)

MFI provides a service for the resolution of conflict and disputes through its referral service. Parties can draw upon the forum's network of over a hundred independent mediators to resolve a dispute.

Contact details

c/o Bea House, Milltown Park, Dublin 6;
www.mediationforumireland.com/01-8175229

Electronic Consumer Dispute Resolution

ECODIR is a free service that helps consumers and businesses to resolve their complaints and disputes online. The process used is negotiation and, if required, mediation, and it all takes place in a private and secure online environment.

Contact details

ECODIR Secretariat, UCD School of Law, University College Dublin, Dublin 4, Ireland; www.ecodir.org

Glossary of Terms

Amendment to Statutory Instrument/directive (EU)
An amendment is a revision or update to a piece of legislation.

Arbitration
Arbitration is a consensual procedure for the settlement of disputes in which both parties agree to be bound by the decision of the arbitrator. The arbitrator's decision is final and is legally binding on both parties. In Ireland arbitration is governed by the Arbitration Acts 1954-98.

Directive (EU)
A directive is a legislative act of the European Union. Agreed by the Council of Ministers it is legally binding and must be passed into national law by all Member States within a certain defined period.

Mediation
Mediation is a process for resolving disputes in which both parties agree to use a neutral party to aid agreement. The terms of agreement are decided by the parties rather than by the mediator. Such an agreement is not legally binding or enforceable through the courts but can be put into a legally binding format.

Recommendation (EU)
A recommendation does not have legal force but is a document to be negotiated and voted on, put forward by the European Commission in the preparation of legislation.

Redress

Redress can be defined as a remedy; to put right a wrong or grievance.

Regulation

A regulation is a legislative Act of the European Union. It is immediately enforceable as law in all Member States simultaneously on the date prescribed and doesn't require any national laws to be introduced first.

Statutory body

A statutory body is an organisation established by statute (legislation).

Statutory Instrument

The Irish statute book consists both of Acts of the Oireachtas and Statutory Instruments. A Statutory Instrument (SI) is a piece of legislation defined by the Statutory Instrument Act 1947 as an 'order, regulation, rule, scheme or bye-law made in exercise of a power conferred by statute'. It is sometimes referred to as 'secondary legislation' or 'delegated legislation'. When, for example, a piece of EU legislation comes into force it can be transposed into Irish law by means of a Statutory Instrument.